JAY SHAFER'S DIY BOOK OF BACKYARD SHEDS & TINY HOUSES

JAY SHAFER

with the Editors of Skills Institute Press

Massive Craftsman-style detailing gives the little Gifford a majestic presence.

JAY SHAFER'S DIY BOOK OF BACKYARD SHEDS & TINY HOUSES

Build Your Own Guest Cottage, Writing Studio,
Home Office, Craft Workshop, or Personal Retreat

JAY SHAFER

with the Editors of Skills Institute Press

FOUR LIGHTS
TINY HOUSE COMPANY

© 2013 by Skills Institute Press LLC and Four Lights Tiny House Company

Published and distributed in North America by Fox Chapel Publishing Company, Inc., East Petersburg, PA.

Jay Shafer's DIY Book of Backyard Sheds & Tiny Houses (ISBN 978 1-56523-816-9, 2013) Is a revised edition of *Tumbleweed DIY Book of Backyard Sheds & Tiny Houses* (ISBN 978-1-56523-704-9, 2012), both published by Fox Chapel Publishing Company, Inc.

Portions of text and art previously published by and reproduced under license with Direct Holdings Americas Inc.

ISBN 978-1-56523-816-9

To learn more about the other great books from Fox Chapel Publishing,
or to find a retailer near you, call toll-free 800-457-9112 or visit us at
www.FoxChapelPublishing.com.

Note to Authors: We are always looking for talented authors to write new books. Please send a brief letter describing your idea to
Acquisition Editor, 1970 Broad Street, East Petersburg, PA 17520.

Printed in China
First printing

TABLE OF CONTENTS

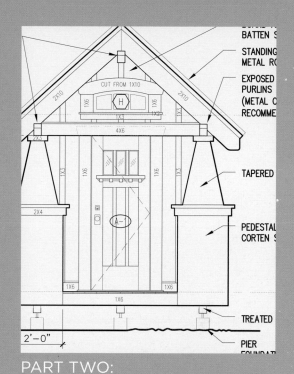

The Gifford makes a welcome and cozy retreat alongside this frozen creek. Tiny buildings like this can be placed almost anywhere.

PART ONE:
COMMITTED TO LESS

BY JAY SHAFER OF FOUR LIGHTS TINY HOUSE COMPANY

A nicely detailed eyebrow window graces the front of the Gifford.

A TINY REVOLUTION

I've spent the better part of the past fifteen years living in houses smaller than some closets, and I've loved it. Mortgage-free living has allowed me to spend my life more or less as I please. Most of my newfound time is put into making little dwellings for others and into exploring how super-sized housing affects ecosystems, economies, and our lives.

It's encouraging to see the small house message embraced by so many. When I finished writing the first edition of *The Small House Book* in 1999 it was one of just three books available on the subject. Now entire shelves are devoted to this new genre. Since forming my first company in 2000, I have watched the nationwide tiny house "industry" grow from my one company to more than a dozen. More encouraging yet, in 2005 the average size of new American houses decreased for the first time in a half-century. It now seems likely that this interest in smaller real estate is not a passing trend, but that our fascination with enormousness may have been. The biggest challenge to the building of smaller houses in North America continues to be prohibitions against it. These restrictions are created primarily by America's housing, lumber, and insurance industries. Once established, they're adopted by states as code and handed off to local governments for fine-tuning and enforcement. All parties involved benefit by ensuring that no American is allowed to live in a house that's too small.

Rather than fighting these entrenched regulations directly, it seems the most expedient means to sustainability may be found in the code's generous loopholes. Most notably, one can often legally build oneself a simple little structure by classifying it as a "vehicle", a "shed" or as "temporary". The question of whether or not you can "live" in your "shed" or "trailer" on your particular piece of land is then left up to the local zoning department who will most likely tell you that you can't, but that you're welcome to "camp out" there as much as you'd like.

Creating sheds and trailers (and even houses) for folks who wish to live simply is what I do best, and it's what this book is about.

The Anderjack (page 20)

BOX BUNGALOWS

Prohibition isn't the only hurdle facing architects striving to create more efficient housing. The real work starts when trying to fit people and their stuff (with elbowroom and safe egress to spare) into a small container and making it the sort of place someone would want to call home. Most challenging of all is trying to determine and accommodate the particular needs of occupant(s).

At its best, creating a small house is a lot like tailoring a suit. One design does not fit all. Pool tables, pools, and gun turrets are all things I've had clients list as necessary to their homes. Things get increasingly difficult when creating stock plans. Making an intricate abode that meets the average person's needs is difficult when there's really no such thing as the average person.

My new Box Bungalows are designed to meet such varied needs with variable design. The series is comprised of six portable shells of a little less than 120 square feet each. A shell can be purchased for as little as $12,000 USD then customized by its owner through the addition of windows, interior components and even more Box Bungalows. Bathroom and kitchen components can be slid through the front door and installed where desired.

The Beavan (page 26)

The Gifford (page 32)

The Stamper (page 38)

The Weller (page 44)

Unitized proportions and varied window options ensure a good fit in hundreds of configurations. Once outfitted, a one-bedroom, single bathroom home could cost less than $20,000 USD. These buildings also make great studios, guesthouses, and sheds.

The structures embody the same classical geometry, anthropometrics, and archetypal form of good design. Traditional Craftsman bungalows, like the ones in this collection, are distinguished by their exposed structural elements, massive columns, broad eaves and by the Movement's intention to make thoughtful design available to ordinary people.

Undue expense and red tape have been cut to keep the Box Bungalows user friendly and affordable. Most municipalities mandate that a permit isn't required to put a building of less than 120 square feet on your property, though you'd want to check with your local building and zoning departments to be sure. While you're at it, see if there are any setback requirements that govern where a structure can be set or how it can be officially used.

The Zinn (page 50)

Home Office/Studio
Guest Room/Marital Aid

Yoga Studio
Pouting Shed

Cottage B

Storage Shed

Cottage A

Spare B.R./Marital Aid

Studio/Guest House

Spare B.R./Guest Room/
Marital Aid

Studio/Guest House

Cottage C

Cottage

Guest house, teen retreat, yoga studio, craft workshop, granny cottage, music room. These floor plans show a few of the infinite ways you could divide and customize the interior of a Box Bungalow. Even a tiny kitchen and bathroom will fit with elbowroom to spare.

Cottage

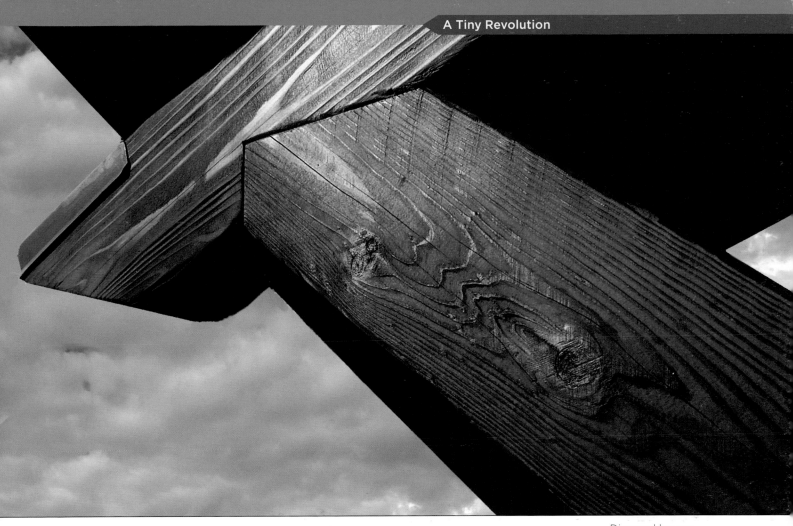

Diagonal braces support the extended purlins of the Gifford and visually frame the front porch.

BROTHELS AND BUNKHOUSES

While my early designs were intended for full-time habitation, it quickly became clear that these little buildings would be used in countless ways. Requests have ranged from spare bedroom to brothel and from bunker to bunkhouse. Yoga studios, workshops, music rooms, and recording studios, home offices, or waterside cabanas also come to mind. Workspaces sometimes do double duty as getaway cottages through the use of foldaway beds.

A building containing a kitchen and bathroom generally needs plumbing, heat, and electricity. These can be as simple as a hose or a rainwater collection system, passive solar, or an RV heater and photovoltaic panels, or a simple extension cord. In studios and workshops, a large refillable water bottle and space heater might be enough. Connecting to the sewer can get expensive. That's why I prefer low-maintenance composting toilets and grey water gardening.

As my life has evolved so have the ways that I use my own tiny residence. After more than a decade of living in less than 100 square feet, I got married and had a baby boy. These events led to the purchase of a 500 square foot house for the family. It is next to this larger structure that my little house now stands. I spend most of my waking hours here, designing more houses and writing about socially responsible, environmentally sustainable shelter. Sometimes I sleep here when my son won't let me sleep next door, and guests sometimes stay here when they come to town. I still call this home, but it's really part of a larger compound household. I'd love to build more little dwellings in the yard for extended family and friends.

Every Box Bungalow comes with a covered porch, board-&-batten cladding, mesa red metal standing seam roofing, mesa red aluminum window cladding, 2 x 6 floor framing, 2 x 3 wall framing, 2 x 4 roof framing, 1 x 3 T&G fir flooring, and 9' cathedral ceilings.

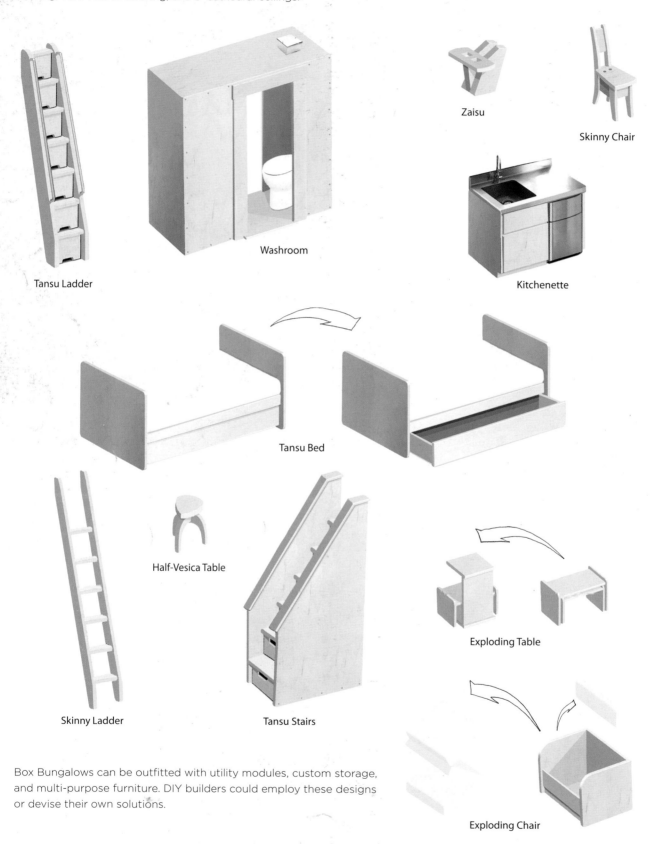

Tansu Ladder

Washroom

Zaisu

Skinny Chair

Kitchenette

Tansu Bed

Half-Vesica Table

Skinny Ladder

Tansu Stairs

Exploding Table

Exploding Chair

Box Bungalows can be outfitted with utility modules, custom storage, and multi-purpose furniture. DIY builders could employ these designs or devise their own solutions.

THE PLANS

I figure that if the house you're creating is very small, you might as well put some of the time and money saved on square footage into good design and quality materials. In fact, in a tiny house, good design becomes all the more important. There's little margin for error and less for waste. The plans on the following pages show overall dimensions and basic construction details for the Box Bungalows, plus a door-and-window schedule. Exterior cladding is board-and-batten; windows are insulated, aluminum-clad low-e; I prefer metal roofs because they're durable, shed the elements readily, and (unlike shingles) won't blow off if the house is taken to the open road. All elements are sized to minimize construction waste and make the best use of materials. I recommend using expanded polystyrene panels with metal foil on one side for insulation. It's affordable, easy to install, much thinner than the equivalent amount of fiberglass, and doesn't need a separate vapor barrier.

A lot of folks reading this will be eagerly creating their own small buildings with their own design sensibilities in mind. For those interested in building one of my Box Bungalows, please visit *www.fourlightshouses.com* for our most up-to-date plans and offerings. In the second half of this book you'll find a how-to introduction guide for constructing cabins and small buildings. I think you'll find it useful whether you go with my plans, or start from scratch.

Great details make all the difference. The custom entry door shown above features high-quality hardware and a speakeasy with glass insert.

This Dickinson Marine stainless steel propane-fired heater, manufactured for use on boats, is more than adequate for these tiny spaces.

Three tiny houses parked in Manhattan give passers-by a double take. HGTV used these shells as the canvas for an interiors bake-off on the popular Design Stars show.

Rear view of Box Bungalows.

FINISHING THE INTERIOR

Once you've got a shell, the interior fittings and finishes are entirely up to you. I've provided layout suggestions on page 12. You could add a modular bathroom and kitchen that could be slid in through the door. Our company has prototyped a 22 ¾" x 66" x 77 ½" bathroom that includes a composting toilet, shower and medicine cabinet. A stainless steel sink/tub/shower option could replace the shower for folks 6' and under. The kitchen is 22 ½" x 42 ½" x 37". It includes a sink, 3.2 cubic foot refrigerator, and a stainless steel countertop. An adjoining stainless steel propane-powered range or hotplate are also available.

A sleeping loft can be set on the collar ties overhead with ease, or you may choose to put a bed down stairs. There are some great Murphy beds and other foldaway furniture on view at *resourcefurniture.com*. I like to include a lot of storage in my spaces and open up one area as much as possible for a sense of volume. Built-ins are also a great way to maximize space.

In spring 2011, three of my Box Bungalows were delivered to a parking lot in Manhattan and handed over to HGTV for use on the network's Design Star. They were just shells when we delivered them: a Beaven, an Anderjack, and a Gifford. Contestants on the show were invited to finish the interiors. It was exciting to see what could be done in just a few hours and wonderful to see our three little houses against the Manhattan skyline (opposite).

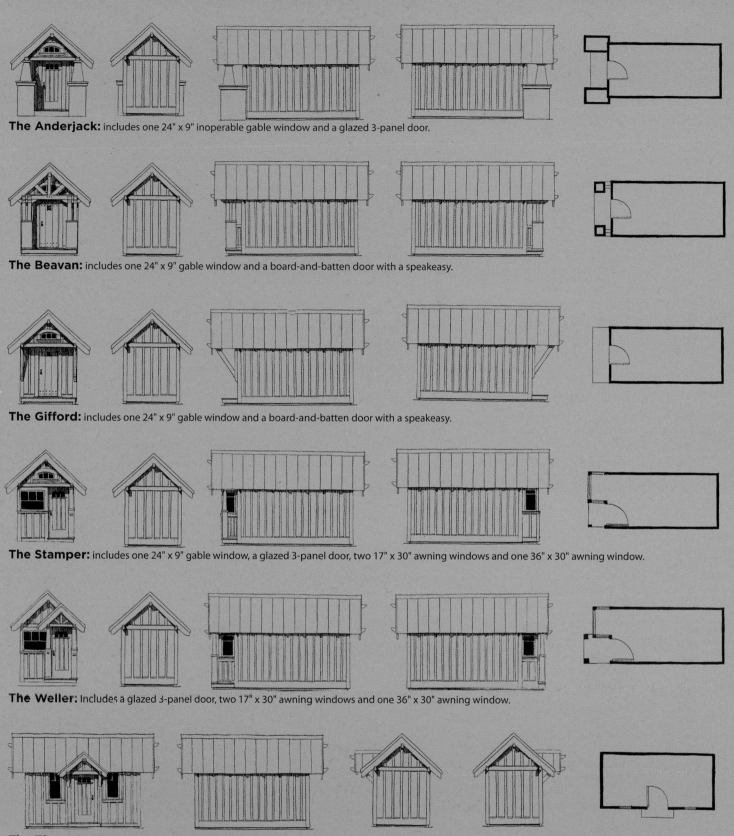

The Anderjack: includes one 24" x 9" inoperable gable window and a glazed 3-panel door.

The Beavan: includes one 24" x 9" gable window and a board-and-batten door with a speakeasy.

The Gifford: includes one 24" x 9" gable window and a board-and-batten door with a speakeasy.

The Stamper: includes one 24" x 9" gable window, a glazed 3-panel door, two 17" x 30" awning windows and one 36" x 30" awning window.

The Weller: Includes a glazed 3-panel door, two 17" x 30" awning windows and one 36" x 30" awning window.

The Zinn: includes a glazed 3-panel door flanked by two 24" x 30" casement windows.

This diagram highlights the differences among the six Box Bungalows. The Anderjack, Beavan, and Gifford feature a centered entry door with distinctive column and purlin treatments in the Craftsman style. The Stamper and the Weller feature an off-center entry door that creates an alcove inside.

The Zinn places the entry door on the long side, sheltered by a gable porch and flanked by two windows. These six versions represent the Box Bungalow series. The newest versions of tiny bungalow plans can be purchased from the Four Lights website, *www.fourlightshouses.com.*

PART TWO:

PLANS FOR TINY HOUSES AND BOX BUNGALOWS

BY JAY SHAFER OF FOUR LIGHTS TINY HOUSE COMPANY

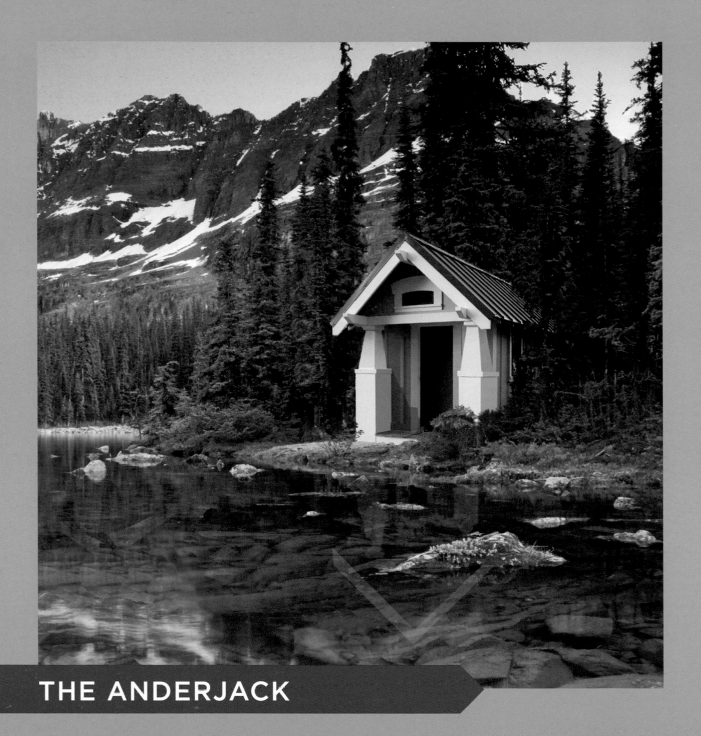

THE ANDERJACK

Set alongside an alpine lake, this little structure measures in at just 112 square feet, not including the loft. The main entry is centered on one end, flanked by two massive columns which, together with the oversized purlins, eave, and window trim, put it squarely in the Craftsman tradition.

Front Elevation

9'-4"
BETWEEN RAFTER EDGES

EXPOSED 4X6 PURLINS (METAL CAP RECOMMENDED)

BOARD AND BATTEN SIDING

STANDING SEAM METAL ROOF

EXPOSED 4X6 PURLINS (METAL CAP RECOMMENDED)

CUT FROM 1X10

2X10

1X1   H   1X6   1X1

2X10

1X3

4X6

2X3

1X3   1X6   1X6   1X3

2X4

A-1

TAPERED COLUMN

PEDESTAL- CORTEN STEEL

1X6   1X6

1X6

TREATED 4X4'S

2'-0"

PIER FOUNDATION

T.O. RIDGE

3'-9 1/2"

LOFT LEVEL

11'-2"

6'-10 1/4"

MAIN FLOOR

B.O. FRAMING

6 1/4"

2'-8"

6'-6 3/4"

3'-10 3/4"

Back Elevation

9'-4"
BETWEEN RAFTER EDGES

EXPOSED 4X6 PURLINS (METAL CAP RECOMMENDED)

STANDING SEAM METAL ROOF

EXPOSED 4X6 PURLINS (METAL CAP RECOMMENDED)

2X10

2X10

2X6

1X4

1X6

G

1X6

1X6   2X2

1X4

1X3 TYPICAL

LP SMARTSIDE OR EQUIVALENT TRIM AND BATTS

LP SMARTSIDE NO GROOVE PANELS OR EQUIVALENT APPLIED VERTICALLY

1X12

TREATED 4X4'S

PIER FOUNDATION

T.O. RIDGE

3'-9 1/2"

LOFT LEVEL

11'-2"

6'-10 1/4"

MAIN FLOOR

B.O. FRAMING

6 1/4"

Side Elevation-Left

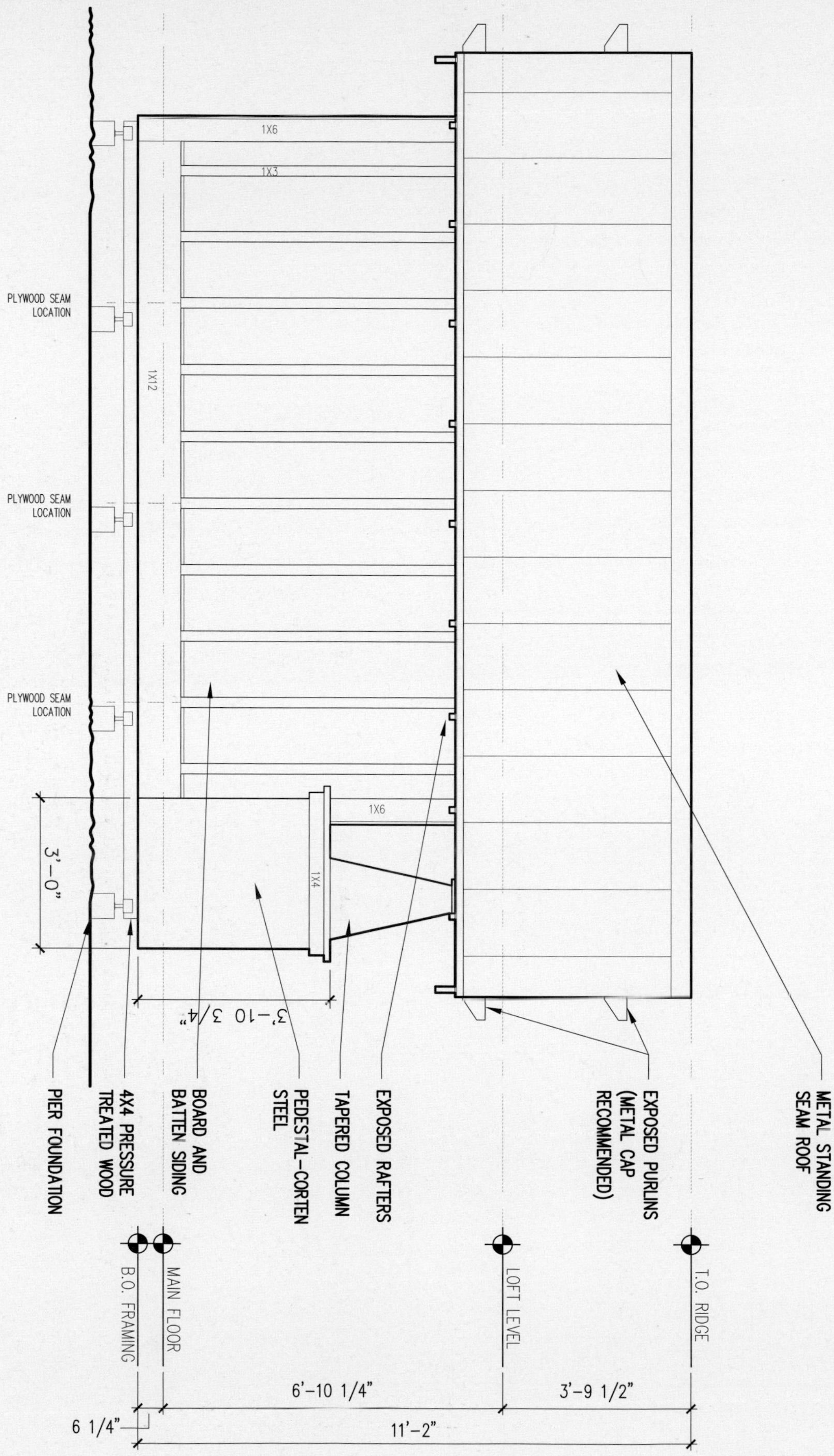

1X6

1X3

1X12

PLYWOOD SEAM
LOCATION

PLYWOOD SEAM
LOCATION

PLYWOOD SEAM
LOCATION

3'-0"

1X6

1X4

3'-10 3/4"

PIER FOUNDATION

4X4 PRESSURE
TREATED WOOD

BOARD AND
BATTEN SIDING

PEDESTAL–CORTEN
STEEL

TAPERED COLUMN

EXPOSED RAFTERS

EXPOSED PURLINS
(METAL CAP
RECOMMENDED)

METAL STANDING
SEAM ROOF

B.O. FRAMING

MAIN FLOOR

LOFT LEVEL

T.O. RIDGE

6'-10 1/4"

3'-9 1/2"

6 1/4"

11'-2"

Side Elevation-Right

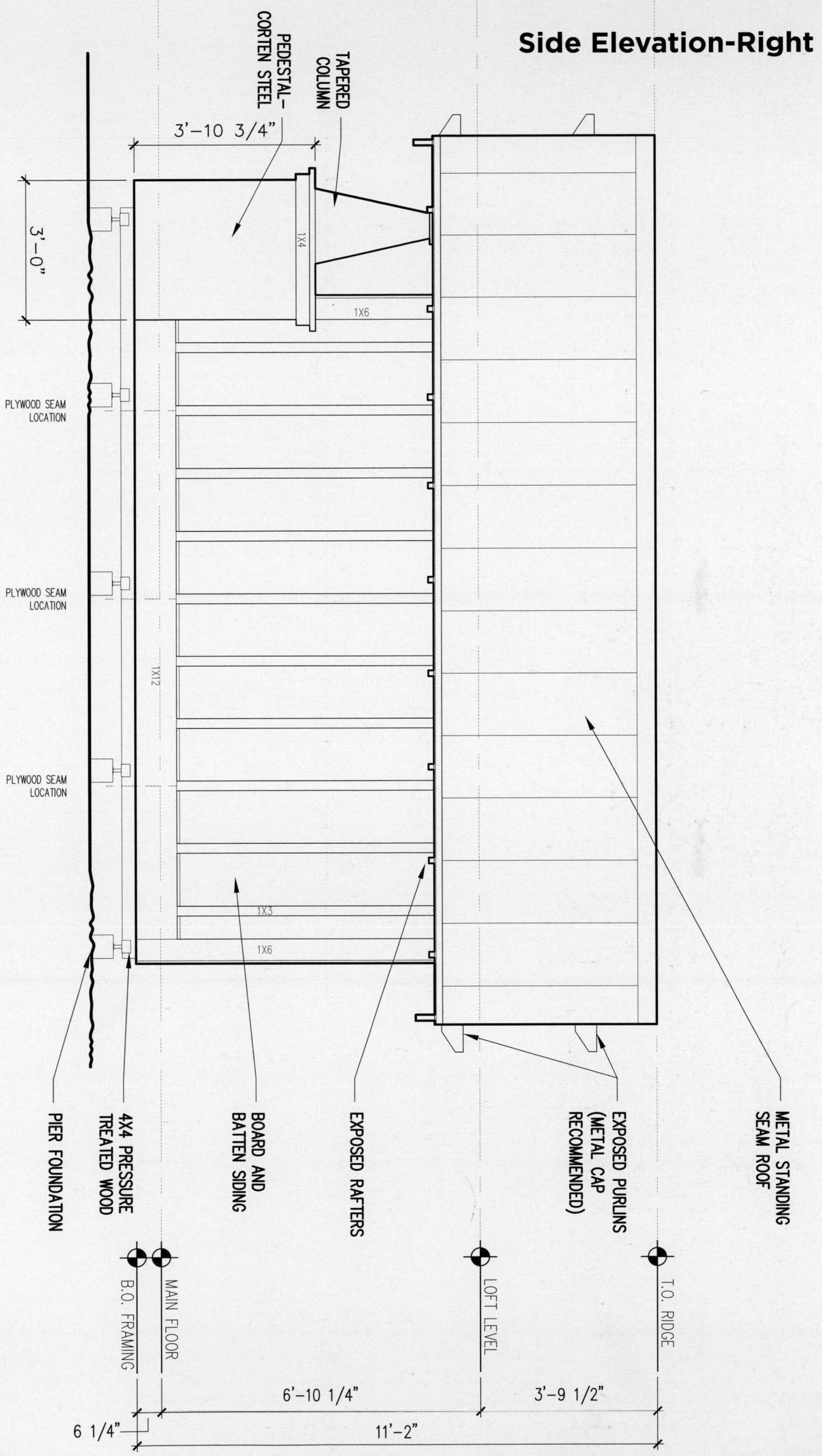

PEDESTAL-
CORTEN STEEL

TAPERED
COLUMN

3'–10 3/4"

1X4

3'–0"

1X6

PLYWOOD SEAM
LOCATION

PLYWOOD SEAM
LOCATION

1X12

PLYWOOD SEAM
LOCATION

1X3

1X6

METAL STANDING
SEAM ROOF

EXPOSED PURLINS
(METAL CAP
RECOMMENDED)

EXPOSED RAFTERS

BOARD AND
BATTEN SIDING

4X4 PRESSURE
TREATED WOOD

PIER FOUNDATION

B.O. FRAMING

MAIN FLOOR

LOFT LEVEL

T.O. RIDGE

6'–10 1/4"

3'–9 1/2"

6 1/4"

11'–2"

Floor Plan

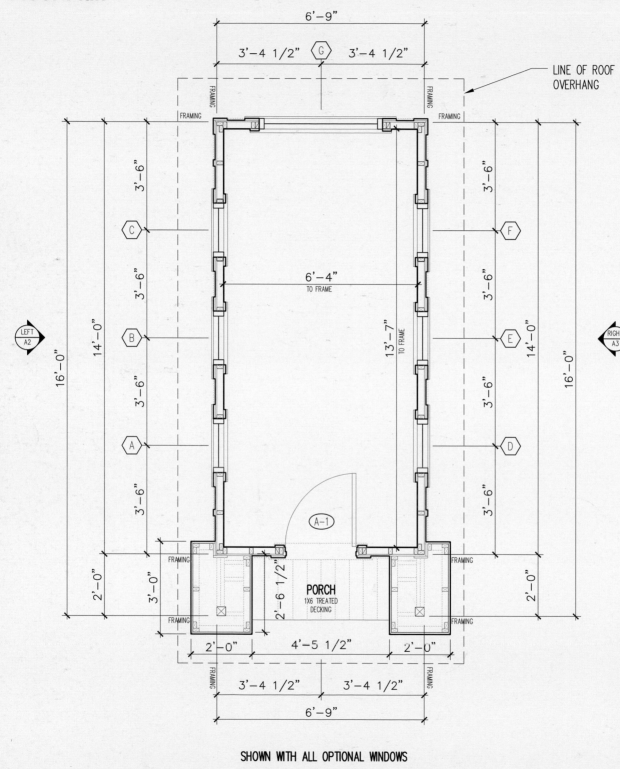

BACK
A1.2

6'-9"

3'-4 1/2" G 3'-4 1/2"

LINE OF ROOF
OVERHANG

FRAMING   FRAMING   FRAMING   FRAMING

3'-6"   3'-6"

C   F

6'-4"
TO FRAME

3'-6"   3'-6"

B   E

16'-0"   14'-0"   13'-7"
TO FRAME   14'-0"   16'-0"

LEFT
A2

RIGHT
A3

3'-6"   3'-6"

A   D

3'-6"   3'-6"

A-1

FRAMING   FRAMING

2'-0"   3'-0"   2'-6 1/2"   PORCH   2'-0"
1X6 TREATED
DECKING

FRAMING   FRAMING

2'-0"   4'-5 1/2"   2'-0"

FRAMING   FRAMING

3'-4 1/2"   3'-4 1/2"

6'-9"

SHOWN WITH ALL OPTIONAL WINDOWS

FRONT
A1.1

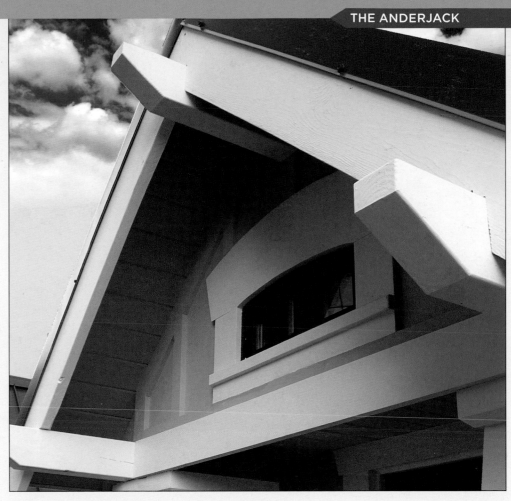

The Anderjack features massive purlins and a Craftsman-style gable window.

Components for The Anderjack :

WINDOW OPTIONS:

    A. MARVIN CLAD LOW-E AWNING WINDOW. 3-OVER-1 SDL.
        21" X 31 $\frac{5}{8}$" R.O.

    B. MARVIN CLAD LOW-E AWNING WINDOW. 3-OVER-1 SDL.
        21" X 31 $\frac{5}{8}$" R.O.

    C. MARVIN CLAD LOW-E AWNING WINDOW. 3-OVER-1 SDL.
        21" X 31 $\frac{5}{8}$" R.O.

    D. MARVIN CLAD LOW-E AWNING WINDOW. 3-OVER-1 SDL.
        21" X 31 $\frac{5}{8}$" R.O

    E. MARVIN CLAD LOW-E AWNING WINDOW. 3-OVER-1 SDL.
        21" X 31 $\frac{5}{8}$" R.O

    F. MARVIN CLAD LOW-E AWNING WINDOW. 3-OVER-1 SDL.
        21" X 31 $\frac{5}{8}$" R.O

    G. 3 - MARVIN CLAD LOW-E AWNING WINDOWS · MULTIPLE ASSEMBLY 3-OVER-1 SDL.
        55" X 27 $\frac{5}{8}$" R.O. (18"X28" WINDOWS)

DOOR :

    A-1. FRONT DOOR : CUSTOM MADE - SEE DRAWING A8 FOR DETAILS.

THE BEAVAN

The Beavan is 112 square feet, not including the loft. Like the Anderjack, the Beavan uses oversize gable, purlin, and column details to create the Craftsman aesthetic. The house is perfectly at home in this sylvan setting.

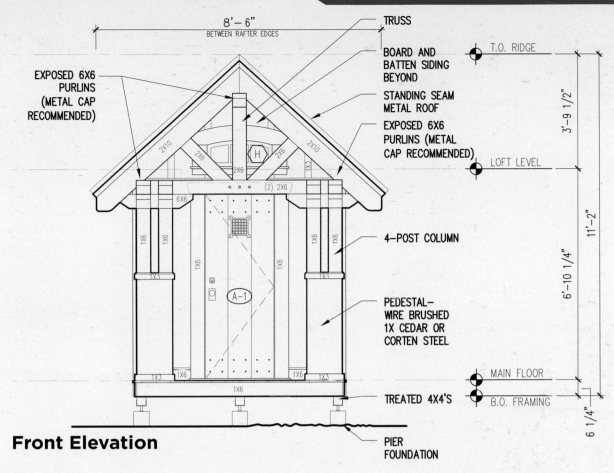

8'-6"
BETWEEN RAFTER EDGES

TRUSS

BOARD AND
BATTEN SIDING
BEYOND

STANDING SEAM
METAL ROOF

EXPOSED 6X6
PURLINS (METAL
CAP RECOMMENDED)

EXPOSED 6X6
PURLINS
(METAL CAP
RECOMMENDED)

4-POST COLUMN

PEDESTAL-
WIRE BRUSHED
1X CEDAR OR
CORTEN STEEL

TREATED 4X4'S

PIER
FOUNDATION

T.O. RIDGE

LOFT LEVEL

MAIN FLOOR

B.O. FRAMING

3'-9 1/2"

6'-10 1/4"

11'-2"

6 1/4"

Front Elevation

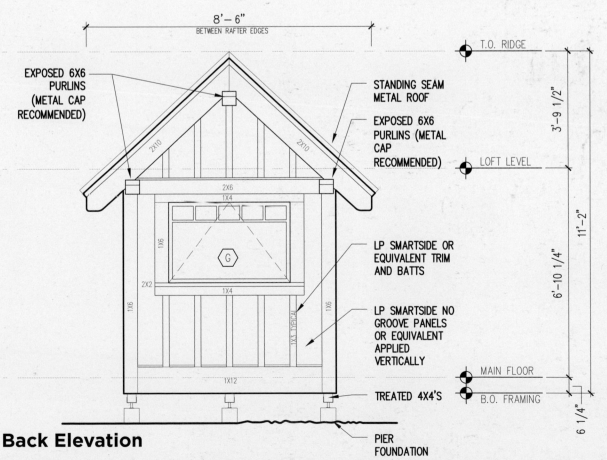

8'-6"
BETWEEN RAFTER EDGES

EXPOSED 6X6
PURLINS
(METAL CAP
RECOMMENDED)

STANDING SEAM
METAL ROOF

EXPOSED 6X6
PURLINS (METAL
CAP
RECOMMENDED)

LP SMARTSIDE OR
EQUIVALENT TRIM
AND BATTS

LP SMARTSIDE NO
GROOVE PANELS
OR EQUIVALENT
APPLIED
VERTICALLY

TREATED 4X4'S

PIER
FOUNDATION

T.O. RIDGE

LOFT LEVEL

MAIN FLOOR

B.O. FRAMING

3'-9 1/2"

6'-10 1/4"

11'-2"

6 1/4"

Back Elevation

Side Elevation-Left

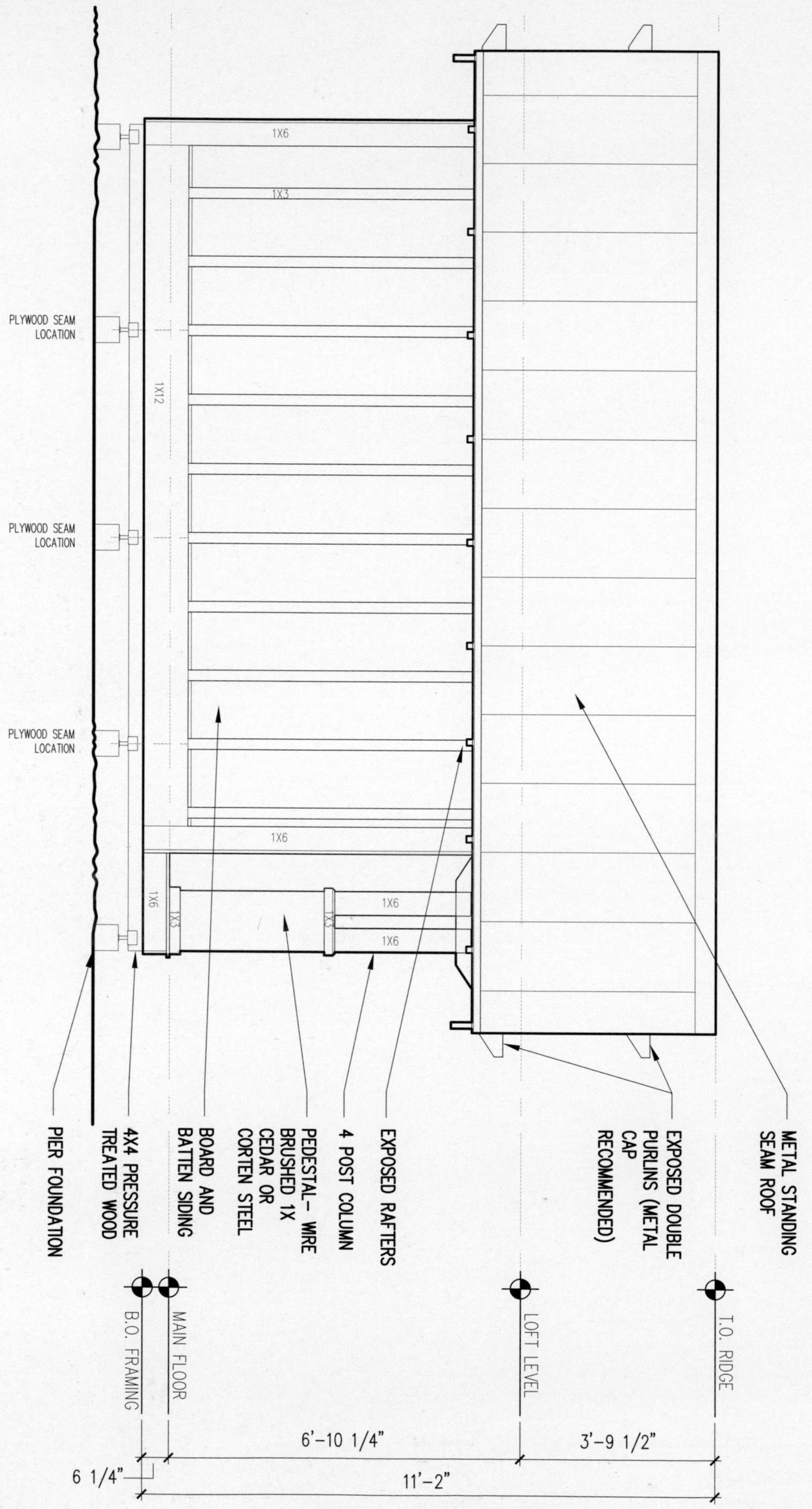

PLYWOOD SEAM
LOCATION

PLYWOOD SEAM
LOCATION

PLYWOOD SEAM
LOCATION

1X6

1X3

1X12

1X6

1X6

1X3

1X6

1X6

PIER FOUNDATION

4X4 PRESSURE
TREATED WOOD

BOARD AND
BATTEN SIDING

PEDESTAL— WIRE
BRUSHED 1X
CEDAR OR
CORTEN STEEL

4 POST COLUMN

EXPOSED RAFTERS

EXPOSED DOUBLE
PURLINS (METAL
CAP
RECOMMENDED)

METAL STANDING
SEAM ROOF

B.O. FRAMING

MAIN FLOOR

LOFT LEVEL

T.O. RIDGE

6'–10 1/4"

3'–9 1/2"

6 1/4"

11'–2"

Side Elevation-Right

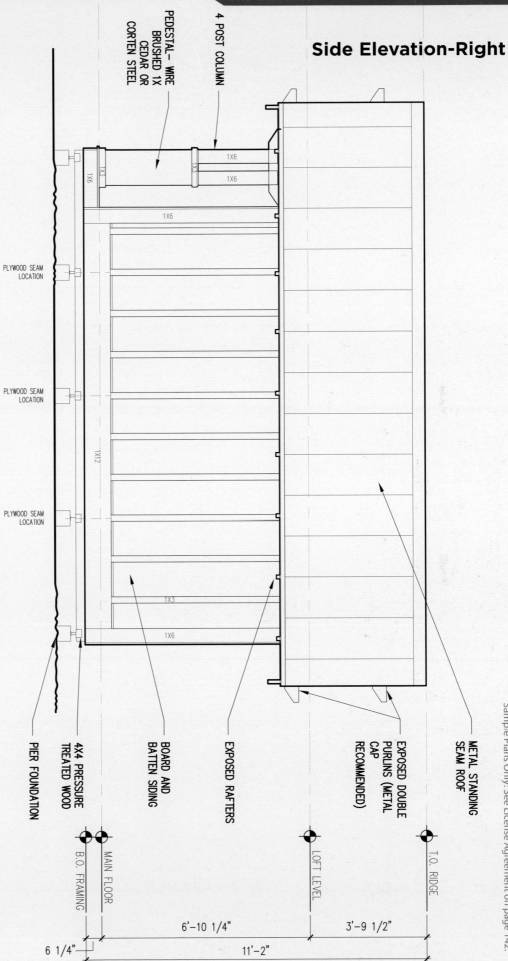

PEDESTAL— WIRE
BRUSHED 1X
CEDAR OR
CORTEN STEEL

4 POST COLUMN

1X3

1X6

1X6

1X6

1X6

1X3

1X12

1X3

1X6

PLYWOOD SEAM
LOCATION

PLYWOOD SEAM
LOCATION

PLYWOOD SEAM
LOCATION

PIER FOUNDATION

4X4 PRESSURE
TREATED WOOD

BOARD AND
BATTEN SIDING

EXPOSED RAFTERS

EXPOSED DOUBLE
PURLINS (METAL
CAP
RECOMMENDED)

METAL STANDING
SEAM ROOF

B.O. FRAMING

MAIN FLOOR

LOFT LEVEL

T.O. RIDGE

6'–10 1/4"

3'–9 1/2"

6 1/4"

11'–2"

Floor Plan

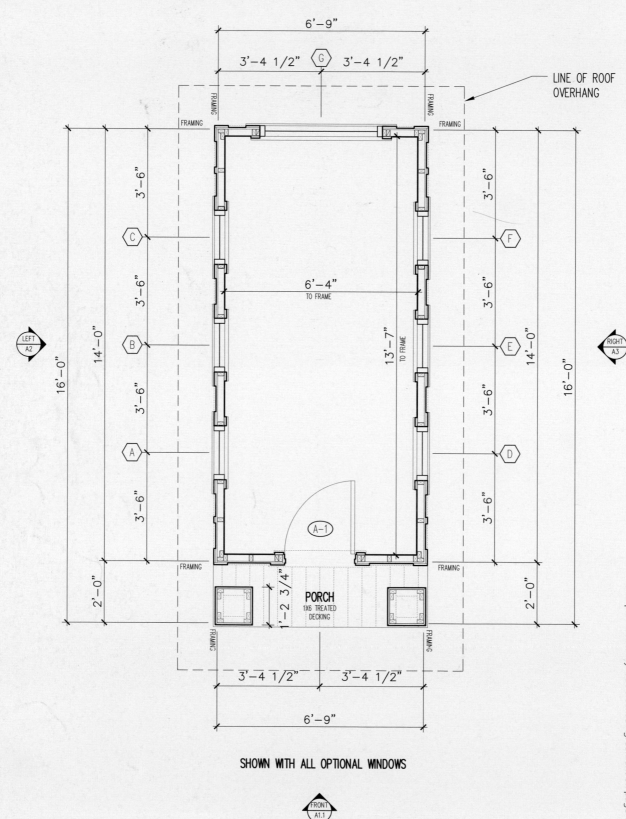

SHOWN WITH ALL OPTIONAL WINDOWS

The Beavan's Craftsman-style gable contrasts strikingly with the Manhattan skyline.

Components for The Beavan :

WINDOW OPTIONS:

    A. MARVIN CLAD LOW-E AWNING WINDOW. 3-OVER-1 SDL.
       21" X 31 ⅝" R.O.

    B. MARVIN CLAD LOW-E AWNING WINDOW. 3-OVER-1 SDL.
       21" X 31 ⅝" R.O.

    C. MARVIN CLAD LOW-E AWNING WINDOW. 3-OVER-1 SDL.
       21" X 31 ⅝" R.O.

    D. MARVIN CLAD LOW-E AWNING WINDOW. 3-OVER-1 SDL.
       21" X 31 ⅝" R.O

    E. MARVIN CLAD LOW-E AWNING WINDOW. 3-OVER-1 SDL.
       21" X 31 ⅝" R.O

    F. MARVIN CLAD LOW-E AWNING WINDOW. 3-OVER-1 SDL.
       21" X 31 ⅝" R.O

    G. 3 - MARVIN CLAD LOW-E AWNING WINDOWS - MULTIPLE ASSEMBLY 3-OVER-1 SDL.
       55" X 27 ⅝" R.O. (18"X28" WINDOWS)

DOOR :

    A-1. FRONT DOOR : CUSTOM MADE - SEE DRAWING A8 FOR DETAILS.

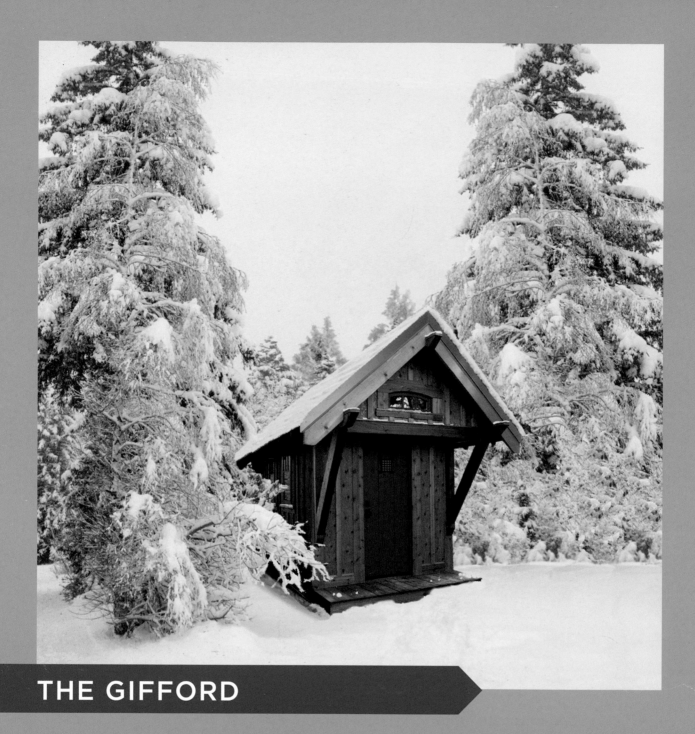

THE GIFFORD

At 7 x 14 feet, the Gifford is just 112 square feet, not including the loft. Like the other tiny houses in this series, it has a durable metal roof that easily sheds snow and ice, standard on Box Bungalows and recommended to amateur builders.

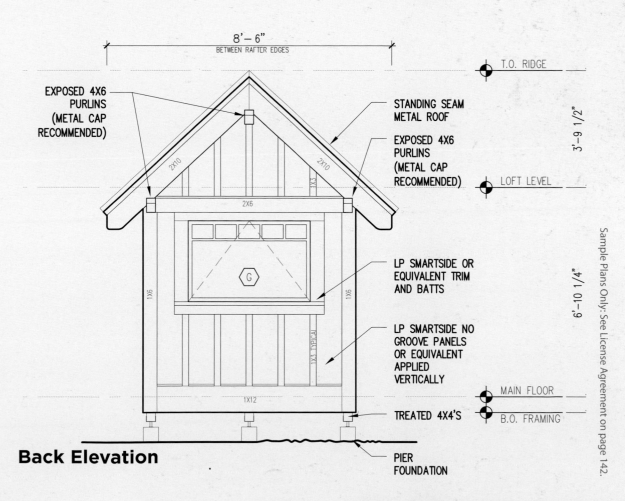

Front Elevation

8'- 6"
BETWEEN RAFTER EDGES

EXPOSED 4X6 PURLINS (METAL CAP RECOMMENDED)

BOARD AND BATTEN SIDING

STANDING SEAM METAL ROOF

EXPOSED 4X6 PURLINS (METAL CAP RECOMMENDED)

BRACE

BOARD AND BATTEN SIDING

TREATED 4X4'S

PIER FOUNDATION

T.O. RIDGE

LOFT LEVEL

MAIN FLOOR

B.O. FRAMING

3'- 9 1/2"

6'-10 1/4"

Back Elevation

8'- 6"
BETWEEN RAFTER EDGES

EXPOSED 4X6 PURLINS (METAL CAP RECOMMENDED)

STANDING SEAM METAL ROOF

EXPOSED 4X6 PURLINS (METAL CAP RECOMMENDED)

LP SMARTSIDE OR EQUIVALENT TRIM AND BATTS

LP SMARTSIDE NO GROOVE PANELS OR EQUIVALENT APPLIED VERTICALLY

TREATED 4X4'S

PIER FOUNDATION

T.O. RIDGE

LOFT LEVEL

MAIN FLOOR

B.O. FRAMING

3'- 9 1/2"

6'-10 1/4"

Side Elevation-Left

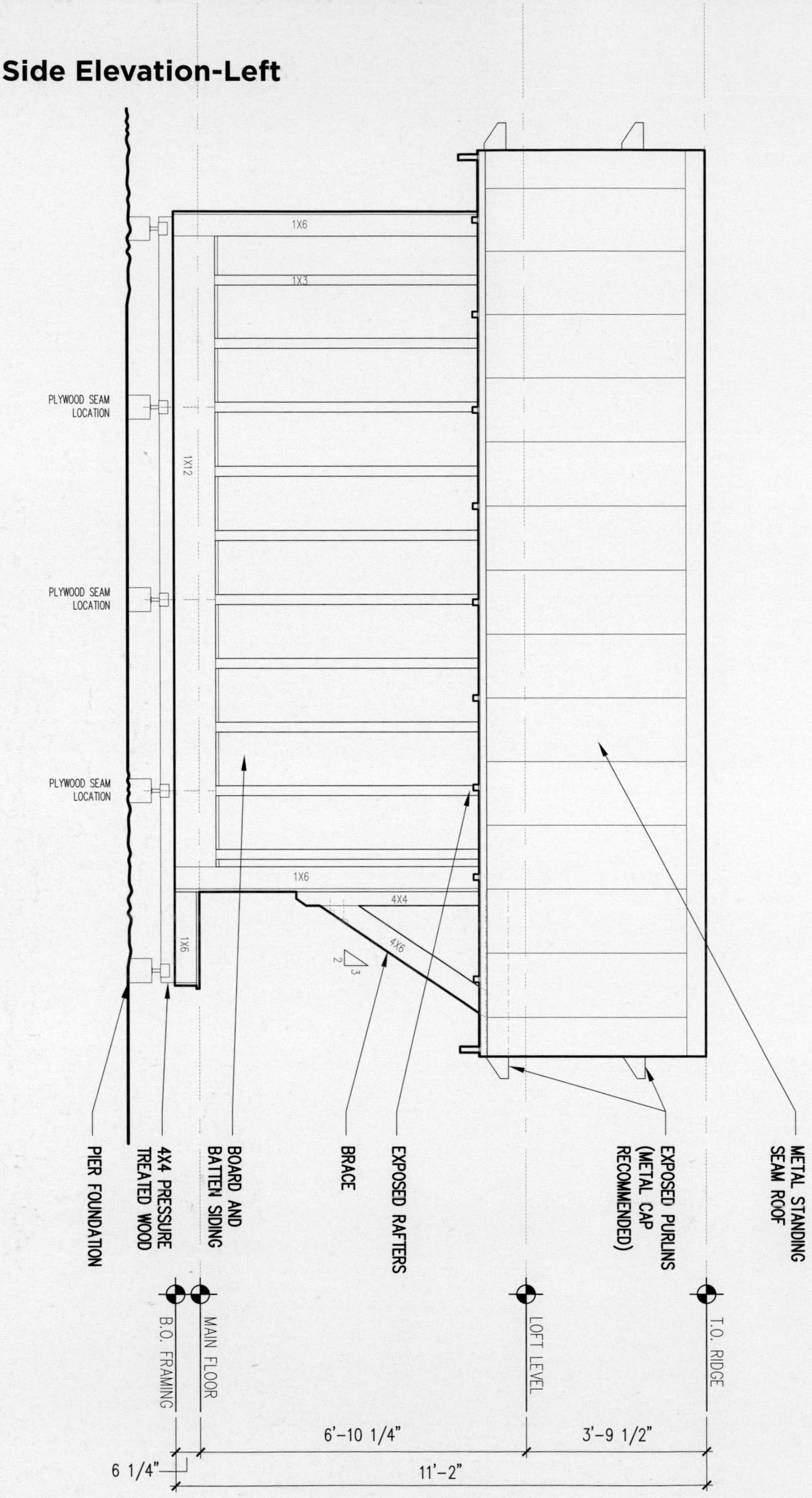

PLYWOOD SEAM
LOCATION

PLYWOOD SEAM
LOCATION

PLYWOOD SEAM
LOCATION

1X6

1X3

1X12

1X6

1X6

4X4

4X6

PIER FOUNDATION

4X4 PRESSURE
TREATED WOOD

BOARD AND
BATTEN SIDING

BRACE

EXPOSED RAFTERS

EXPOSED PURLINS
(METAL CAP
RECOMMENDED)

METAL STANDING
SEAM ROOF

B.O. FRAMING

MAIN FLOOR

LOFT LEVEL

T.O. RIDGE

6'-10 1/4"

3'-9 1/2"

6 1/4"

11'-2"

Side Elevation-Right

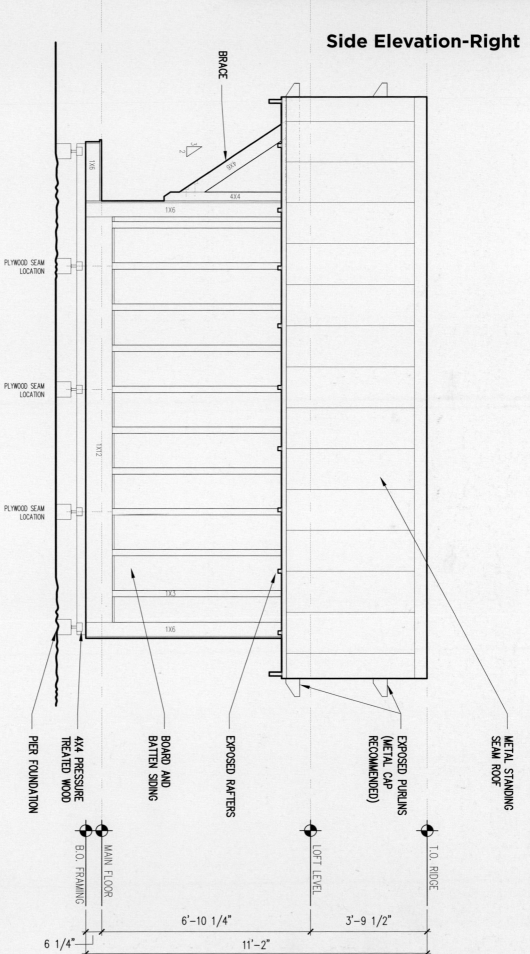

BRACE

PLYWOOD SEAM
LOCATION

PLYWOOD SEAM
LOCATION

PLYWOOD SEAM
LOCATION

1X6

4X6

4X4

1X6

1X12

1X3

1X6

PIER FOUNDATION

4X4 PRESSURE
TREATED WOOD

BOARD AND
BATTEN SIDING

EXPOSED RAFTERS

EXPOSED PURLINS
(METAL CAP
RECOMMENDED)

METAL STANDING
SEAM ROOF

B.O. FRAMING

MAIN FLOOR

LOFT LEVEL

T.O. RIDGE

6'-10 1/4"

3'-9 1/2"

6 1/4"

11'-2"

Floor Plan

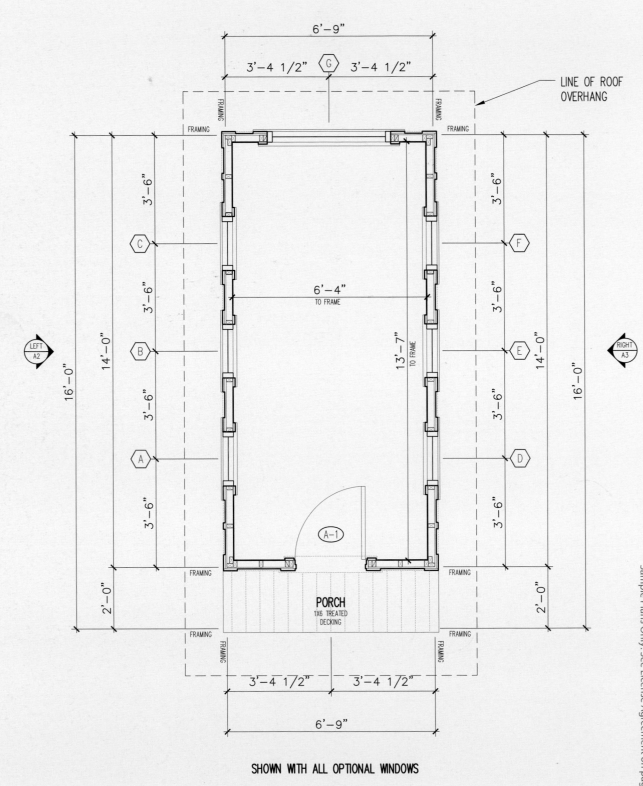

BACK
A1.2

6'-9"

3'-4 1/2"   G   3'-4 1/2"

LINE OF ROOF
OVERHANG

FRAMING   FRAMING

FRAMING   FRAMING

3'-6"   3'-6"

C   F

3'-6"   6'-4"   3'-6"
TO FRAME

14'-0"   14'-0"

LEFT
A2

16'-0"   B   13'-7"   E   16'-0"
TO FRAME

3'-6"   3'-6"

RIGHT
A3

A   D

3'-6"   3'-6"

A-1

FRAMING   FRAMING

2'-0"   2'-0"

FRAMING   FRAMING

PORCH
1X6 TREATED
DECKING

FRAMING   FRAMING

3'-4 1/2"   3'-4 1/2"

6'-9"

SHOWN WITH ALL OPTIONAL WINDOWS

FRONT
A1.1

Rear view of the Gifford in a winter landscape.

Components for Z. Gifford :

WINDOW OPTIONS:

    A. MARVIN CLAD LOW-E AWNING WINDOW. 3-OVER-1 SDL.
        21" X 31 $\frac{5}{8}$" R.O.

    B. MARVIN CLAD LOW-E AWNING WINDOW. 3-OVER-1 SDL.
        21" X 31 $\frac{5}{8}$" R.O.

    C. MARVIN CLAD LOW-E AWNING WINDOW. 3-OVER-1 SDL.
        21" X 31 $\frac{5}{8}$" R.O.

    D. MARVIN CLAD LOW-E AWNING WINDOW. 3-OVER-1 SDL.
        21" X 31 $\frac{5}{8}$" R.O

    E. MARVIN CLAD LOW-E AWNING WINDOW. 3-OVER-1 SDL.
        21" X 31 $\frac{5}{8}$" R.O

    F. MARVIN CLAD LOW-E AWNING WINDOW. 3-OVER-1 SDL.
        21" X 31 $\frac{5}{8}$" R.O

    G. 3 - MARVIN CLAD LOW-E AWNING WINDOWS - MULTIPLE ASSEMBLY 3-OVER-1 SDL.
        55" X 27 $\frac{5}{8}$" R.O. (18"X28" WINDOWS)

DOOR :

    A-1. FRONT DOOR : CUSTOM MADE - SEE DRAWING A8 FOR DETAILS.

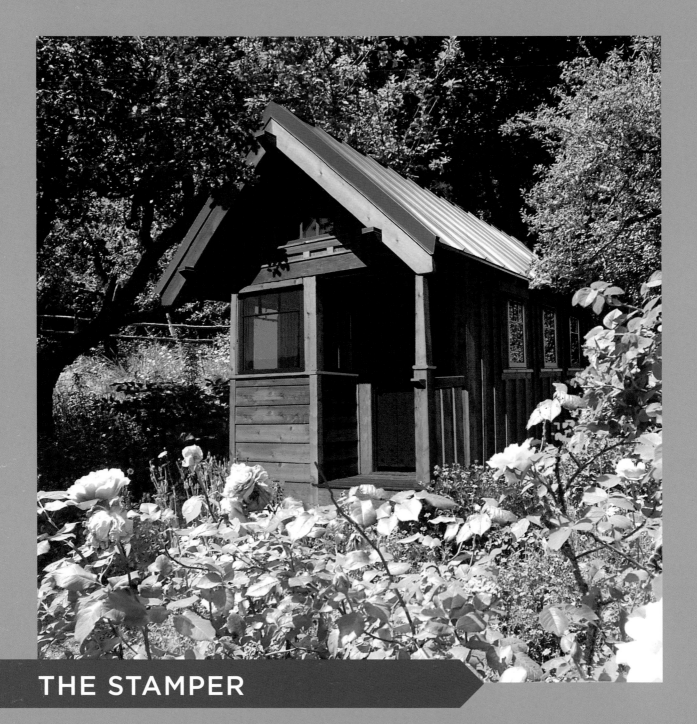

THE STAMPER

Similar in design to the other front-gabled Box Bungalows, the Stamper measures in at a slightly larger 115 square feet, not including the loft. There's an alcove in the main room with windows on three sides. Board-and-batten siding is standard on the Box Bungalows, and recommended to DIY builders.

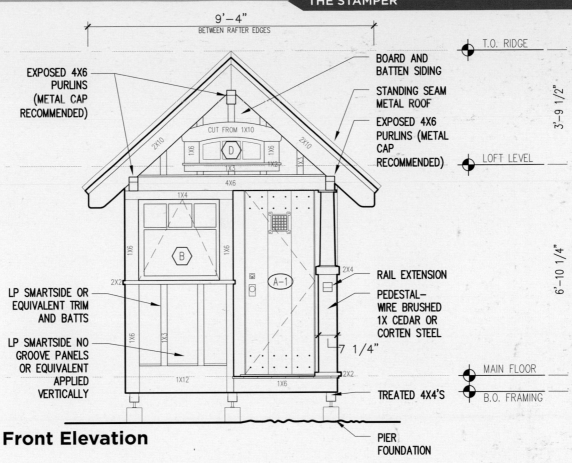

Front Elevation

Front Elevation labels:

- EXPOSED 4X6 PURLINS (METAL CAP RECOMMENDED)
- BOARD AND BATTEN SIDING
- STANDING SEAM METAL ROOF
- EXPOSED 4X6 PURLINS (METAL CAP RECOMMENDED)
- RAIL EXTENSION
- PEDESTAL- WIRE BRUSHED 1X CEDAR OR CORTEN STEEL
- TREATED 4X4'S
- PIER FOUNDATION
- LP SMARTSIDE OR EQUIVALENT TRIM AND BATTS
- LP SMARTSIDE NO GROOVE PANELS OR EQUIVALENT APPLIED VERTICALLY
- 9'-4" BETWEEN RAFTER EDGES
- T.O. RIDGE
- 3'-9 1/2"
- LOFT LEVEL
- 6'-10 1/4"
- MAIN FLOOR
- B.O. FRAMING
- 7 1/4"

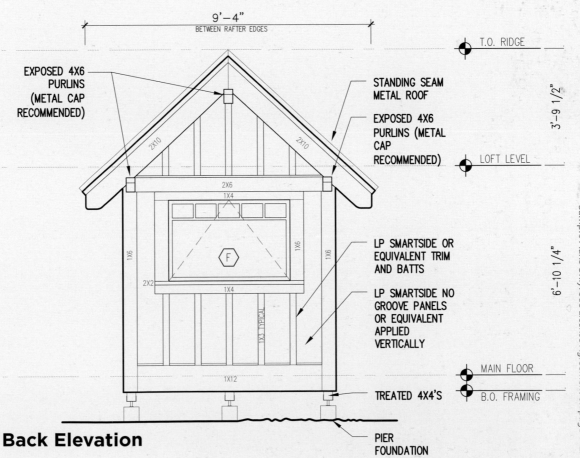

Back Elevation

Back Elevation labels:

- EXPOSED 4X6 PURLINS (METAL CAP RECOMMENDED)
- STANDING SEAM METAL ROOF
- EXPOSED 4X6 PURLINS (METAL CAP RECOMMENDED)
- LP SMARTSIDE OR EQUIVALENT TRIM AND BATTS
- LP SMARTSIDE NO GROOVE PANELS OR EQUIVALENT APPLIED VERTICALLY
- TREATED 4X4'S
- PIER FOUNDATION
- 9'-4" BETWEEN RAFTER EDGES
- T.O. RIDGE
- 3'-9 1/2"
- LOFT LEVEL
- 6'-10 1/4"
- MAIN FLOOR
- B.O. FRAMING

Side Elevation-Left

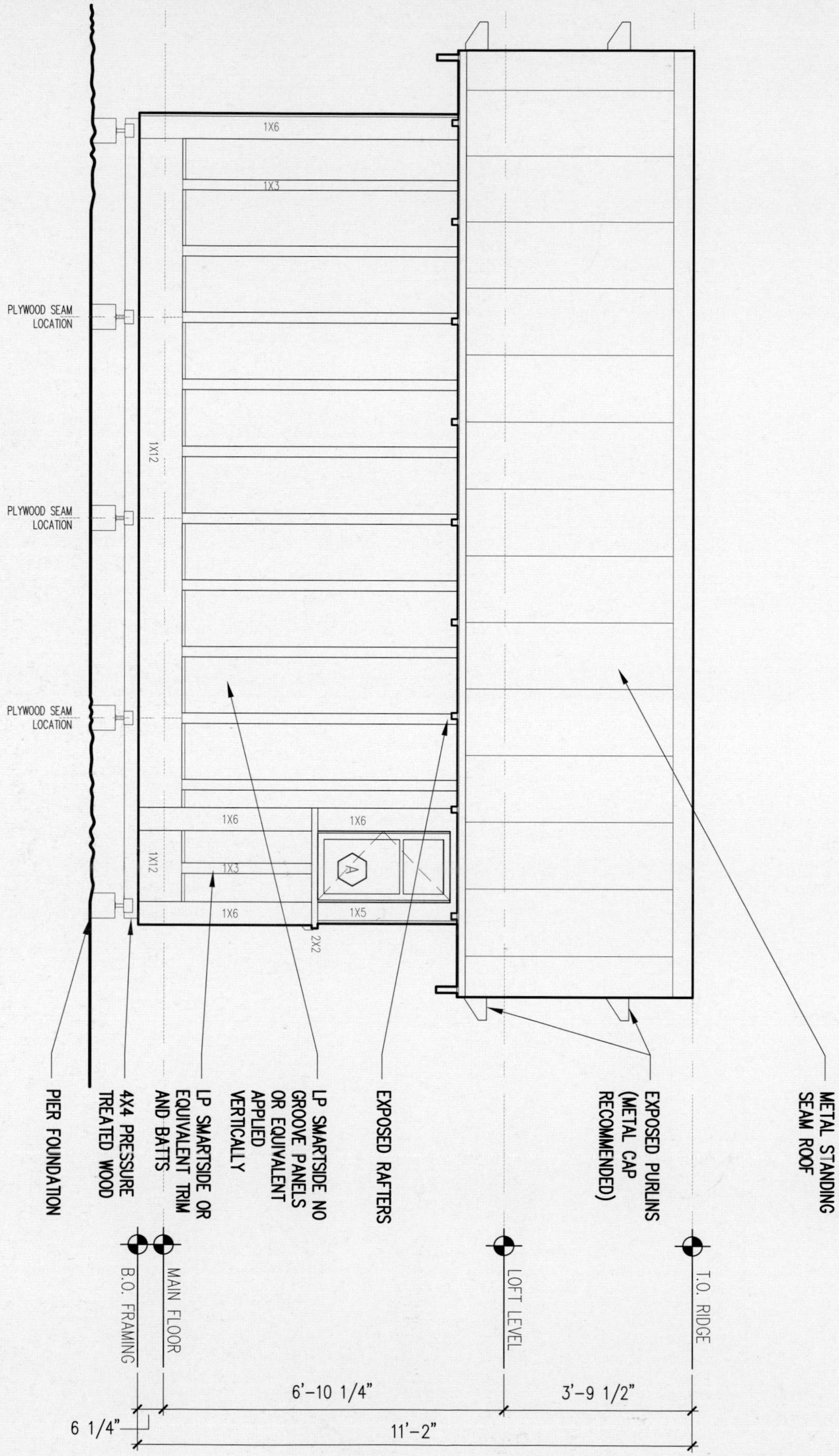

1X6

1X3

1X12

PLYWOOD SEAM
LOCATION

PLYWOOD SEAM
LOCATION

PLYWOOD SEAM
LOCATION

1X6   1X6

1X12   1X3

1X6   1X5

2X2

A

PIER FOUNDATION

4X4 PRESSURE
TREATED WOOD

LP SMARTSIDE OR
EQUIVALENT TRIM
AND BATTS

LP SMARTSIDE NO
GROOVE PANELS
OR EQUIVALENT
APPLIED
VERTICALLY

EXPOSED RAFTERS

EXPOSED PURLINS
(METAL CAP
RECOMMENDED)

METAL STANDING
SEAM ROOF

B.O. FRAMING

MAIN FLOOR

LOFT LEVEL

T.O. RIDGE

6'-10 1/4"   3'-9 1/2"

6 1/4"

11'-2"

Side Elevation-Right

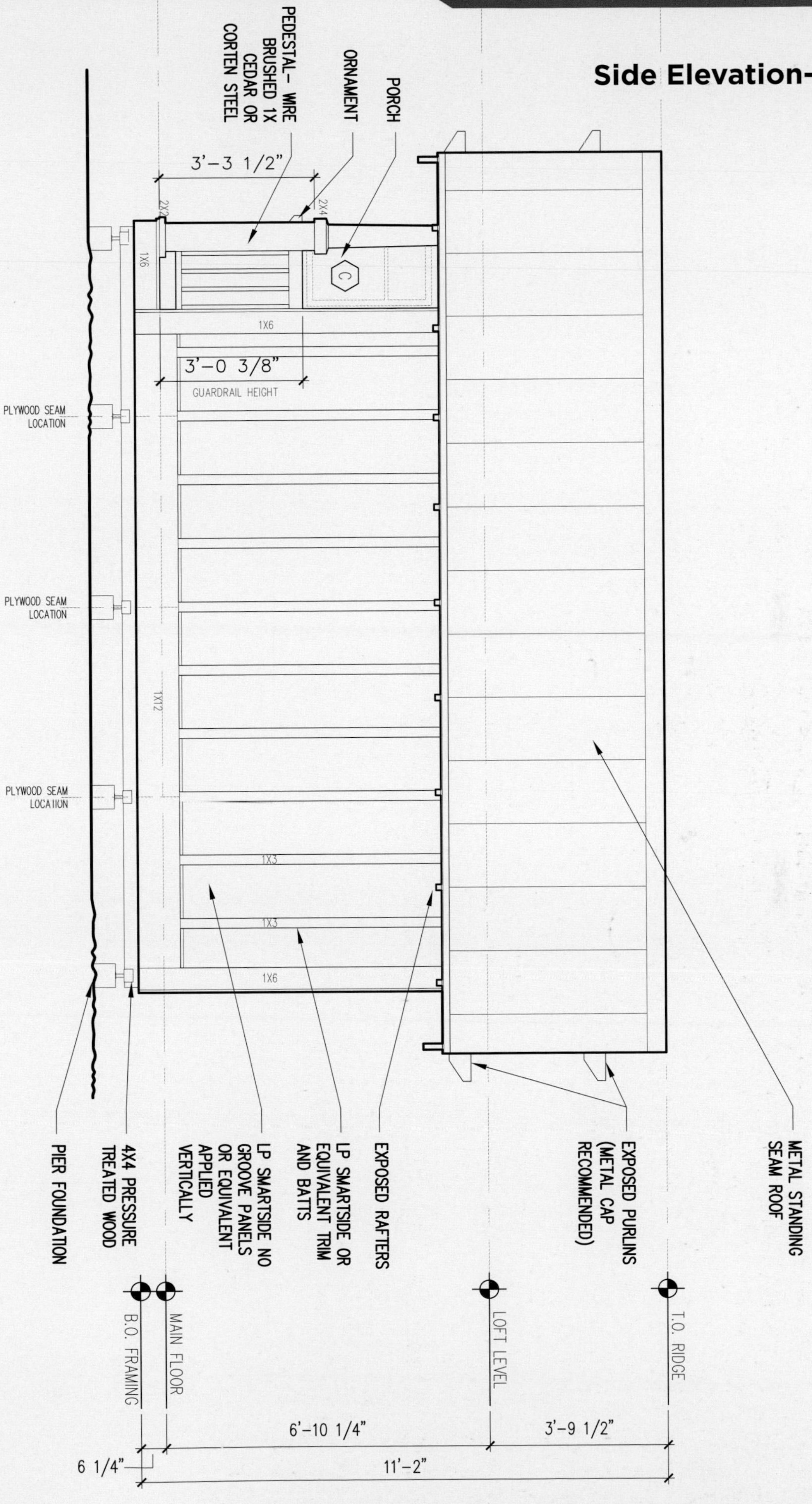

PEDESTAL— WIRE
BRUSHED 1X
CEDAR OR
CORTEN STEEL

ORNAMENT

PORCH

3'–3 1/2"

2X6

2X4

1X6

1X6

3'–0 3/8"

GUARDRAIL HEIGHT

C

PLYWOOD SEAM
LOCATION

PLYWOOD SEAM
LOCATION

PLYWOOD SEAM
LOCATION

1X12

1X3

1X3

1X6

PIER FOUNDATION

4X4 PRESSURE
TREATED WOOD

LP SMARTSIDE NO
GROOVE PANELS
OR EQUIVALENT
APPLIED
VERTICALLY

LP SMARTSIDE OR
EQUIVALENT TRIM
AND BATTS

EXPOSED RAFTERS

EXPOSED PURLINS
(METAL CAP
RECOMMENDED)

METAL STANDING
SEAM ROOF

B.O. FRAMING

MAIN FLOOR

LOFT LEVEL

T.O. RIDGE

6'–10 1/4"

3'–9 1/2"

6 1/4"

11'–2"

Floor Plan

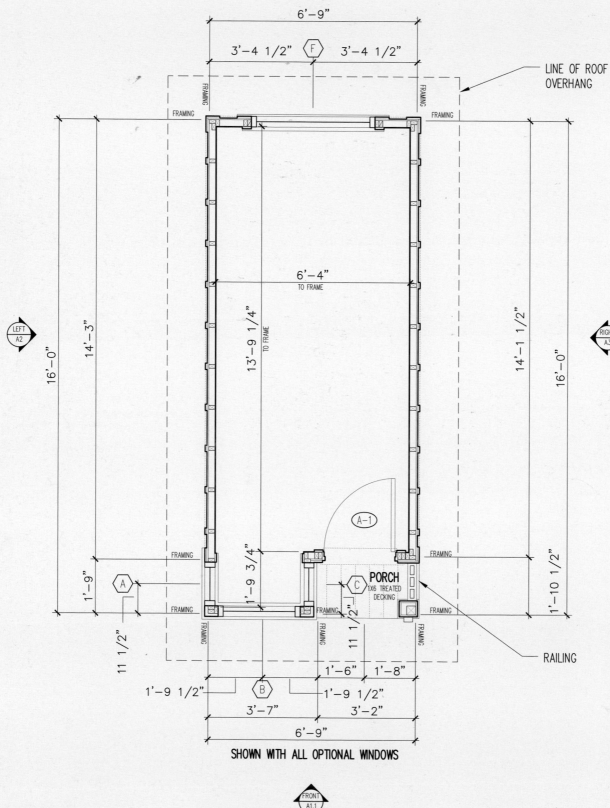

BACK
A1.2

6'-9"

3'-4 1/2" F 3'-4 1/2"

LINE OF ROOF
OVERHANG

FRAMING   FRAMING

FRAMING   FRAMING

LEFT
A2

16'-0"

14'-3"

6'-4"
TO FRAME

13'-9 1/4"
TO FRAME

RIGHT
A3

14'-1 1/2"

16'-0"

A-1

1'-9"

FRAMING

A

1'-9 3/4"

FRAMING

FRAMING

1'-10 1/2"

RAILING

PORCH
1X6 TREATED
DECKING

C

11 1/2"

11 1/2"

FRAMING   FRAMING   FRAMING

11 1/2"

1'-6"   1'-8"

1'-9 1/2"

B

1'-9 1/2"

3'-7"   3'-2"

6'-9"

SHOWN WITH ALL OPTIONAL WINDOWS

FRONT
A1.1

Rear view of the Stamper
in a backyard setting.

Components for The Stamper :

WINDOW OPTIONS:

- A. MARVIN CLAD LOW-E CASEMENT WINDOW. 1-OVER-1 SDL.
  17" X 31 ⅝" R.O.
- B. MARVIN CLAD LOW-E AWNING WINDOW. 3-OVER-1 SDL.
  32" X 31 ⅝"R.O.
- C. MARVIN CLAD LOW-E CASEMENT WINDOW. 1-OVER-1 SDL.
  17" X 31 ⅝" R.O
- D. CUSTOM LOW-E INOPERABLE WINDOW.
  26 ½" X 11" R.O.
- E. (OPTIONAL) CUSTOM LOW-E INOPERABLE WINDOW.
  26 ½" X 11" R.O.
- F. MARVIN CLAD LOW-E AWNING WINDOW. 5-OVER-1 SDL.
  49" X 31 ⅝" R.O.

DOOR :

A-1. FRONT DOOR : CUSTOM. 2'-3¾" X 6'-0"

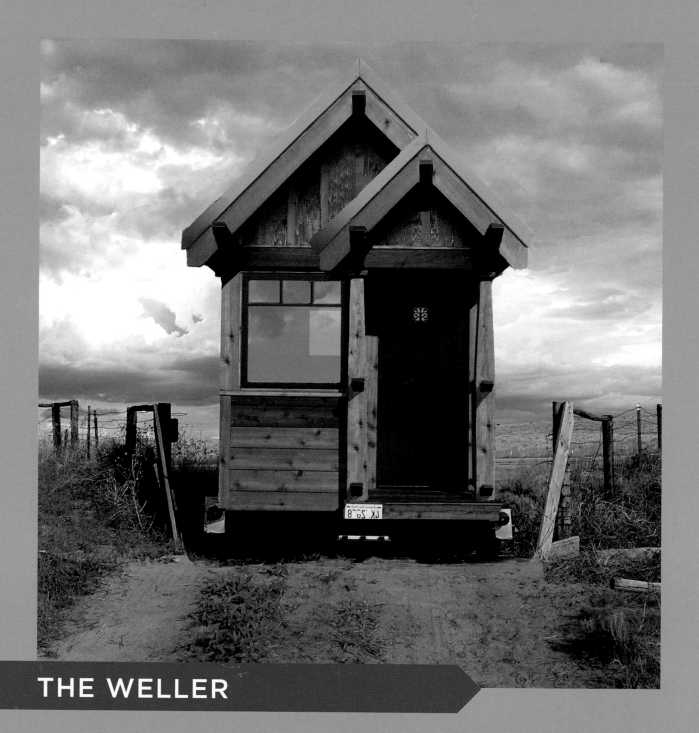

THE WELLER

The Weller, shown here parked in a Colorado alpine meadow, is 115 square feet, not including the loft. The gable over the offset front door gives the Weller a distinctive look as well as some highly useful loft storage inside.

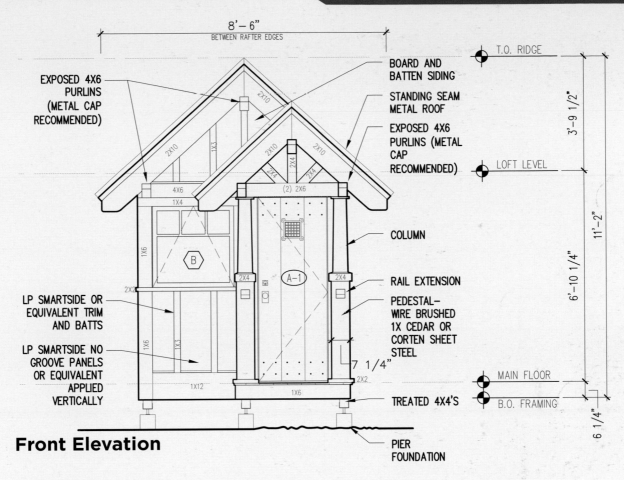

8' – 6"
BETWEEN RAFTER EDGES

EXPOSED 4X6 PURLINS (METAL CAP RECOMMENDED)

BOARD AND BATTEN SIDING

STANDING SEAM METAL ROOF

EXPOSED 4X6 PURLINS (METAL CAP RECOMMENDED)

COLUMN

RAIL EXTENSION

PEDESTAL- WIRE BRUSHED 1X CEDAR OR CORTEN SHEET STEEL

LP SMARTSIDE OR EQUIVALENT TRIM AND BATTS

LP SMARTSIDE NO GROOVE PANELS OR EQUIVALENT APPLIED VERTICALLY

TREATED 4X4'S

PIER FOUNDATION

T.O. RIDGE

3'-9 1/2"

LOFT LEVEL

6'-10 1/4"

11'-2"

MAIN FLOOR

B.O. FRAMING

6 1/4"

7 1/4"

Front Elevation

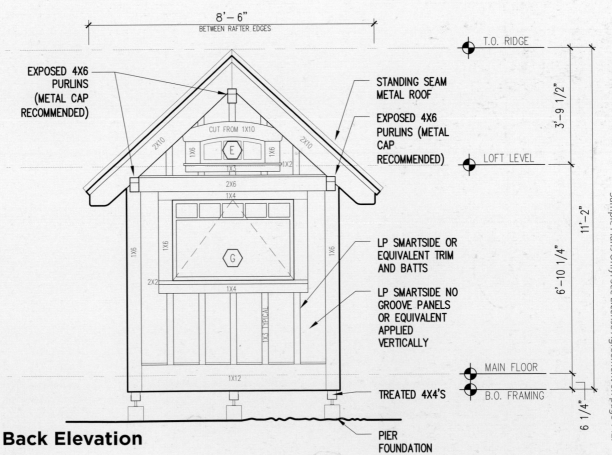

8' – 6"
BETWEEN RAFTER EDGES

EXPOSED 4X6 PURLINS (METAL CAP RECOMMENDED)

STANDING SEAM METAL ROOF

EXPOSED 4X6 PURLINS (METAL CAP RECOMMENDED)

CUT FROM 1X10

LP SMARTSIDE OR EQUIVALENT TRIM AND BATTS

LP SMARTSIDE NO GROOVE PANELS OR EQUIVALENT APPLIED VERTICALLY

TREATED 4X4'S

PIER FOUNDATION

T.O. RIDGE

3'-9 1/2"

LOFT LEVEL

6'-10 1/4"

11'-2"

MAIN FLOOR

B.O. FRAMING

6 1/4"

Back Elevation

Side Elevation-Left

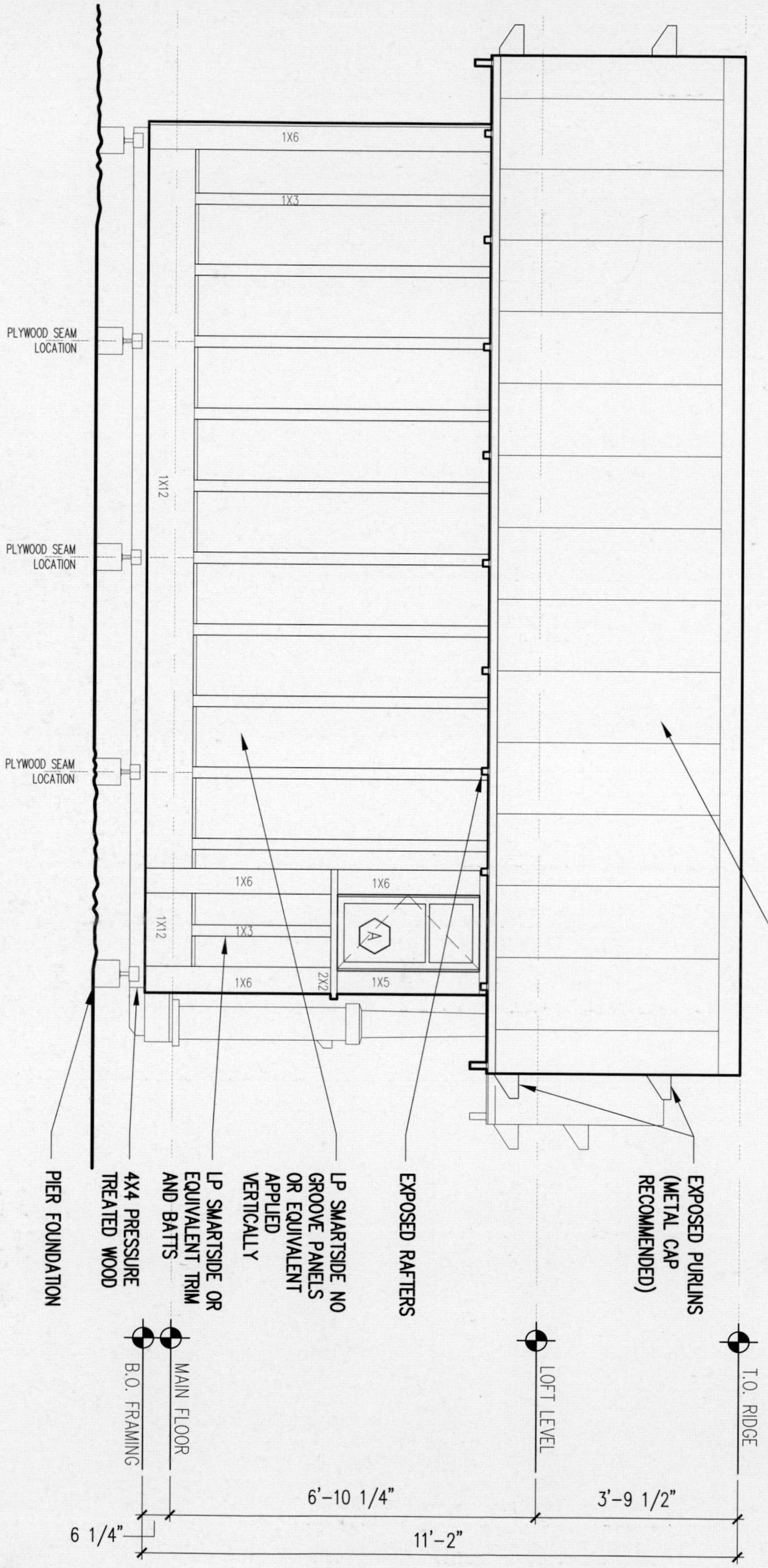

1X6

1X3

1X12

PLYWOOD SEAM
LOCATION

PLYWOOD SEAM
LOCATION

PLYWOOD SEAM
LOCATION

1X6   1X6

1X12

1X3

A

1X6   2X2   1X5

PIER FOUNDATION

4X4 PRESSURE
TREATED WOOD

LP SMARTSIDE OR
EQUIVALENT TRIM
AND BATTS

LP SMARTSIDE OR
EQUIVALENT PANELS
OR EQUIVALENT
APPLIED
VERTICALLY

LP SMARTSIDE NO
GROOVE PANELS
OR EQUIVALENT
APPLIED
VERTICALLY

EXPOSED RAFTERS

EXPOSED PURLINS
(METAL CAP
RECOMMENDED)

METAL STANDING
SEAM ROOF

B.O. FRAMING

MAIN FLOOR

LOFT LEVEL

T.O. RIDGE

6 1/4"

6'-10 1/4"

3'-9 1/2"

11'-2"

Side Elevation-Right

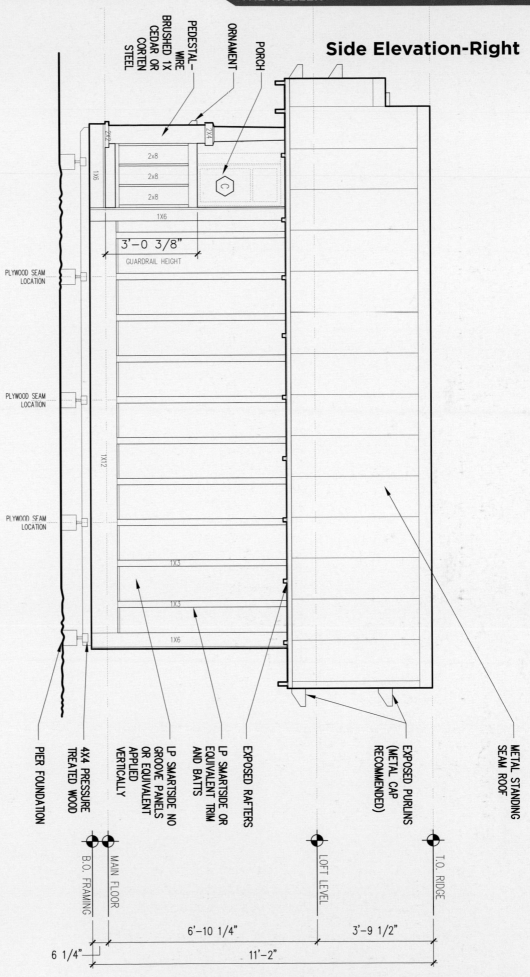

PEDESTAL—
WIRE
BRUSHED 1X
CEDAR OR
CORTEN
STEEL

ORNAMENT

PORCH

2X2

2X4

1X6

2x8

2x8

2x8

C

1X6

3'-0 3/8"

GUARDRAIL HEIGHT

PLYWOOD SEAM
LOCATION

PLYWOOD SEAM
LOCATION

PLYWOOD SEAM
LOCATION

1X12

1X3

1X3

1X6

PIER FOUNDATION

4X4 PRESSURE
TREATED WOOD

LP SMARTSIDE NO
GROOVE PANELS
OR EQUIVALENT
APPLIED
VERTICALLY

LP SMARTSIDE OR
EQUIVALENT TRIM
AND BATS

EXPOSED RAFTERS

EXPOSED PURLINS
(METAL CAP
RECOMMENDED)

METAL STANDING
SEAM ROOF

B.O. FRAMING

MAIN FLOOR

LOFT LEVEL

T.O. RIDGE

6'-10 1/4"

3'-9 1/2"

6 1/4"

11'-2"

Floor Plan

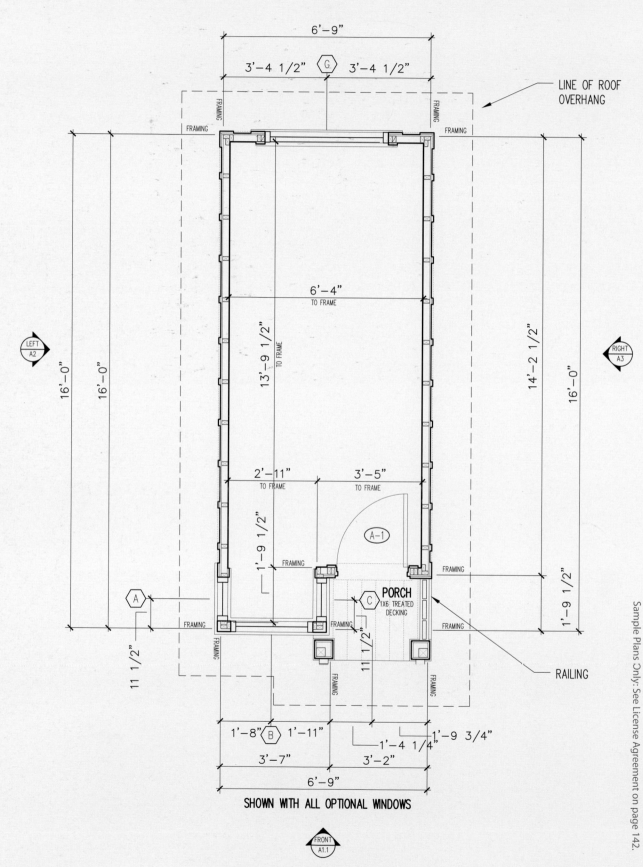

BACK
A1.2

6'-9"

3'-4 1/2" G. 3'-4 1/2"

LINE OF ROOF
OVERHANG

FRAMING   FRAMING

FRAMING   FRAMING

LEFT
A2

RIGHT
A3

16'-0"

16'-0"

6'-4"
TO FRAME

13'-9 1/2"
TO FRAME

14'-2 1/2"

16'-0"

2'-11"
TO FRAME

3'-5"
TO FRAME

A-1

1'-9 1/2"

FRAMING

FRAMING

1'-9 1/2"

A

PORCH
1X6 TREATED
DECKING

C

FRAMING   FRAMING   FRAMING

11 1/2"

FRAMING

11 1/2"

FRAMING   FRAMING

RAILING

1'-8" B 1'-11"

1'-4 1/4" 1'-9 3/4"

3'-7"

3'-2"

6'-9"

SHOWN WITH ALL OPTIONAL WINDOWS

FRONT
A1.1

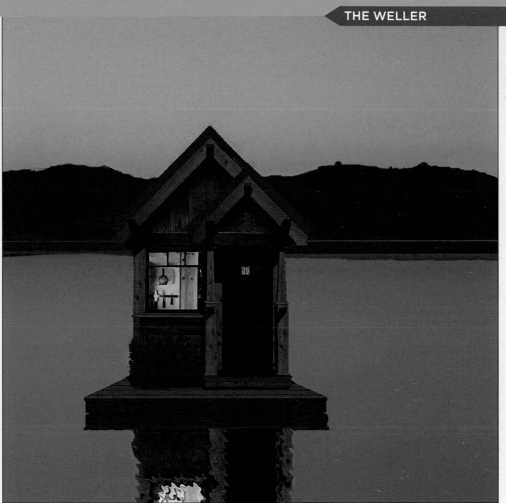

As you can see, tiny houses can sit virtually anywhere.

Components for Weller :

WINDOW OPTIONS:

    A.   MARVIN CLAD LOW-E CASEMENT WINDOW. 1-OVER-1 SDL.
         17" X 31 ⅝" R.O.
    B.   MARVIN CLAD LOW-E AWNING WINDOW. 3-OVER-1 SDL.
         32" X 31 ⅝"R.O.
    C. MARVIN CLAD LOW-E CASEMENT WINDOW. 1-OVER-1 SDL.
         17" X 31 ⅝" R.O
    E.   CUSTOM LOW-E INOPERABLE WINDOW.
         26 ½" X 11" R.O.
    G.   MARVIN CLAD LOW-E AWNING WINDOW. 5-OVER-1 SDL.
         49" X 31 ⅝" R.O.

DOOR :

    A-1. FRONT DOOR : CUSTOM. 2'-3¾" x 6'-0"

THE ZINN

This end-gable design is just 98 square feet, not including the loft. The Zinn features a main entry centered on the long side and flanked by sunny windows, creating new sitting and layout options.

Front Elevation

T.O. RIDGE

LOFT LEVEL

MAIN FLOOR

B.O. FRAMING

11'-2"

3'-9 1/2"

6'-10 1/4"

6 1/4"

METAL STANDING SEAM ROOF

BOARD AND BATTEN SIDING

EXPOSED PURLINS (METAL CAP RECOMMENDED)

EXPOSED RAFTERS

LP SMARTSIDE NO GROOVE PANELS OR EQUIVALENT APPLIED VERTICALLY

LP SMARTSIDE OR EQUIVALENT TRIM AND BATTS

4X4 PRESSURE TREATED WOOD

PIER FOUNDATION

EXPOSED PURLINS (METAL CAP RECOMMENDED)

REMOVABLE AWNING AND BRACE

REMOVABLE PORCH

1X6

1X12

A

2X6

3X6

A-1

6X6

1X3

6X6

1X3

1X5

1X5

B

1X5

2X2

1X3

1X12

1X6

2X6

Back Elevation

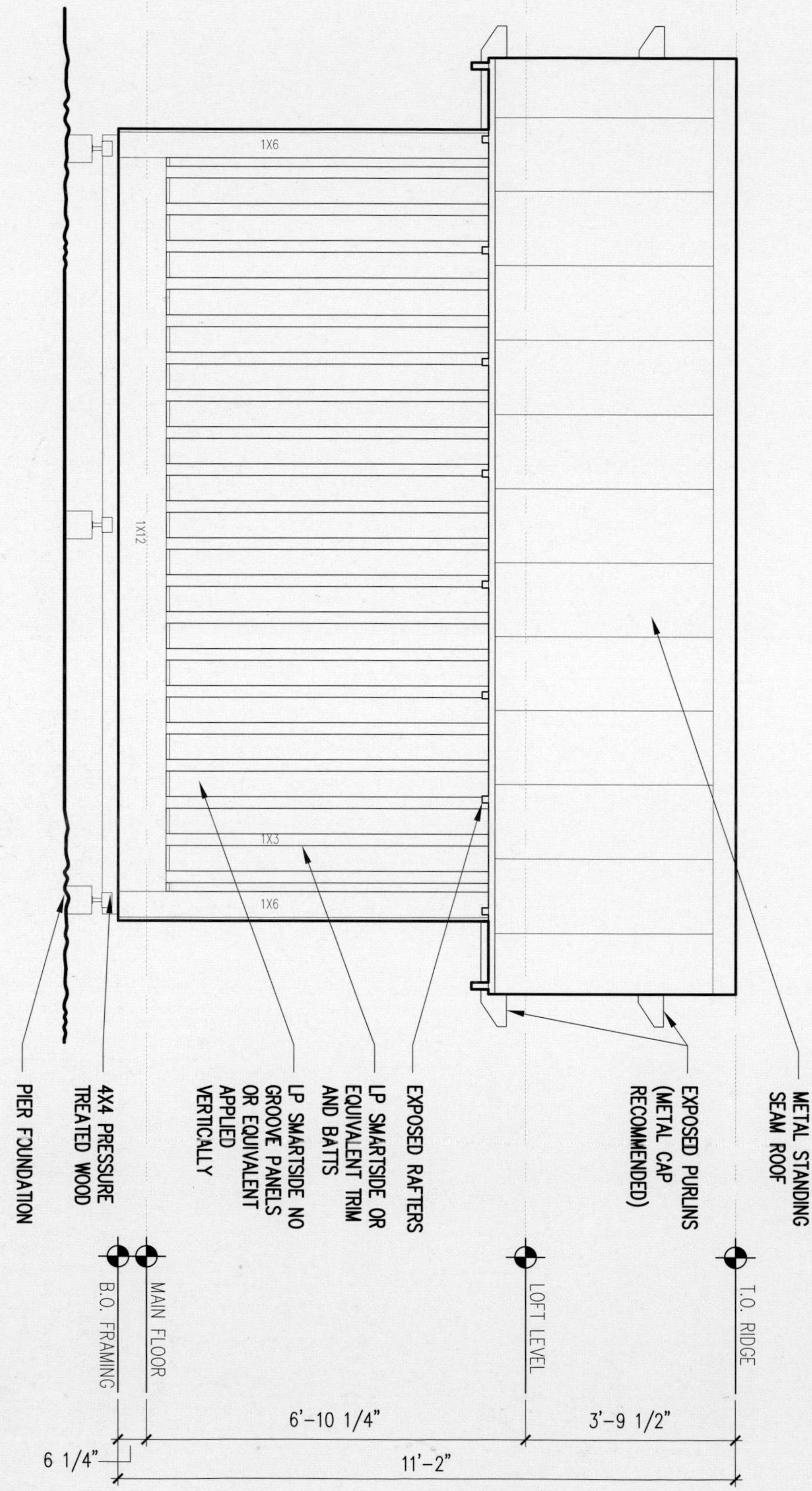

1X6

1X12

1X3

1X6

PIER FOUNDATION

4X4 PRESSURE
TREATED WOOD

LP SMARTSIDE NO
GROOVE PANELS
OR EQUIVALENT
APPLIED
VERTICALLY

LP SMARTSIDE OR
EQUIVALENT TRIM
AND BATTS

EXPOSED RAFTERS

EXPOSED PURLINS
(METAL CAP
RECOMMENDED)

METAL STANDING
SEAM ROOF

B.O. FRAMING

MAIN FLOOR

LOFT LEVEL

T.O. RIDGE

6'–10 1/4"

3'–9 1/2"

6 1/4"

11'–2"

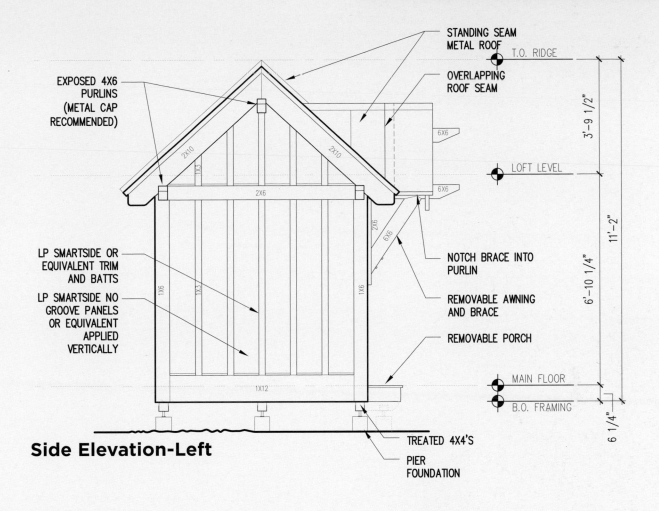

STANDING SEAM
METAL ROOF

EXPOSED 4X6
PURLINS
(METAL CAP
RECOMMENDED)

OVERLAPPING
ROOF SEAM

T.O. RIDGE

6X6

3'-9 1/2"

LOFT LEVEL

6X6

11'-2"

2X10

2X10

2X6

NOTCH BRACE INTO
PURLIN

LP SMARTSIDE OR
EQUIVALENT TRIM
AND BATTS

REMOVABLE AWNING
AND BRACE

6'-10 1/4"

LP SMARTSIDE NO
GROOVE PANELS
OR EQUIVALENT
APPLIED
VERTICALLY

REMOVABLE PORCH

1X6

1X3

1X6

MAIN FLOOR

B.O. FRAMING

1X12

6 1/4"

TREATED 4X4'S

PIER
FOUNDATION

Side Elevation-Left

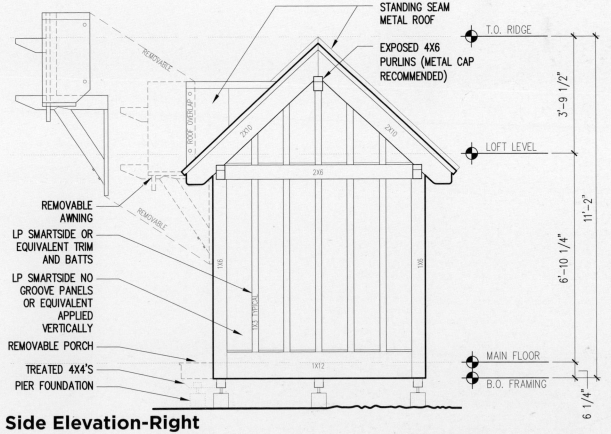

STANDING SEAM
METAL ROOF

EXPOSED 4X6
PURLINS (METAL CAP
RECOMMENDED)

T.O. RIDGE

REMOVABLE

3'-9 1/2"

ROOF OVERLAP

2X10

2X10

LOFT LEVEL

2X6

11'-2"

REMOVABLE
AWNING

REMOVABLE

LP SMARTSIDE OR
EQUIVALENT TRIM
AND BATTS

1X6

1X6

6'-10 1/4"

LP SMARTSIDE NO
GROOVE PANELS
OR EQUIVALENT
APPLIED
VERTICALLY

1X3 TYPICAL

REMOVABLE PORCH

MAIN FLOOR

TREATED 4X4'S

1X12

PIER FOUNDATION

B.O. FRAMING

6 1/4"

Side Elevation-Right

Floor Plan

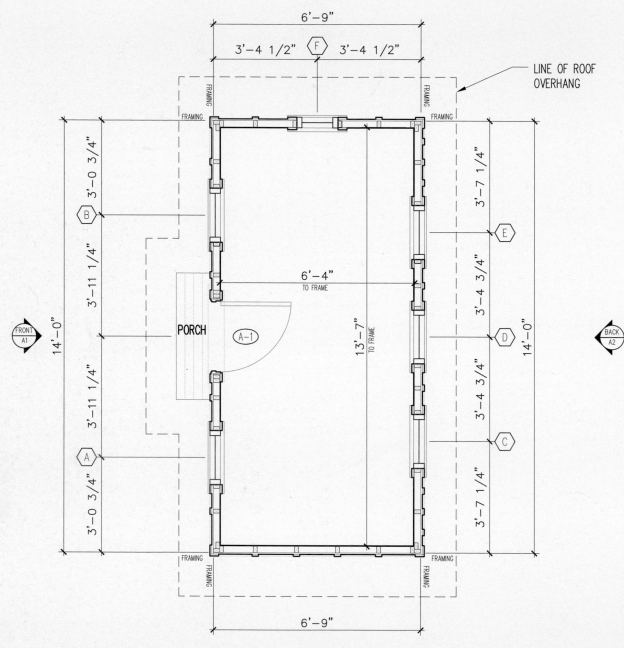

LEFT
A3.1

6'-9"

3'-4 1/2" (F) 3'-4 1/2"

LINE OF ROOF
OVERHANG

FRAMING

FRAMING

FRAMING

FRAMING

3'-0 3/4"

(B)

(E)

3'-7 1/4"

3'-11 1/4"

3'-4 3/4"

6'-4"
TO FRAME

FRONT
A1

PORCH

(A-1)

13'-7"
TO FRAME

(D)

3'-4 3/4"

14'-0"

14'-0"

BACK
A2

3'-11 1/4"

(A)

(C)

3'-7 1/4"

3'-0 3/4"

FRAMING

FRAMING

FRAMING

FRAMING

6'-9"

SHOWN WITH ALL OPTIONAL WINDOWS

RIGHT
A3.2

Roof Plan

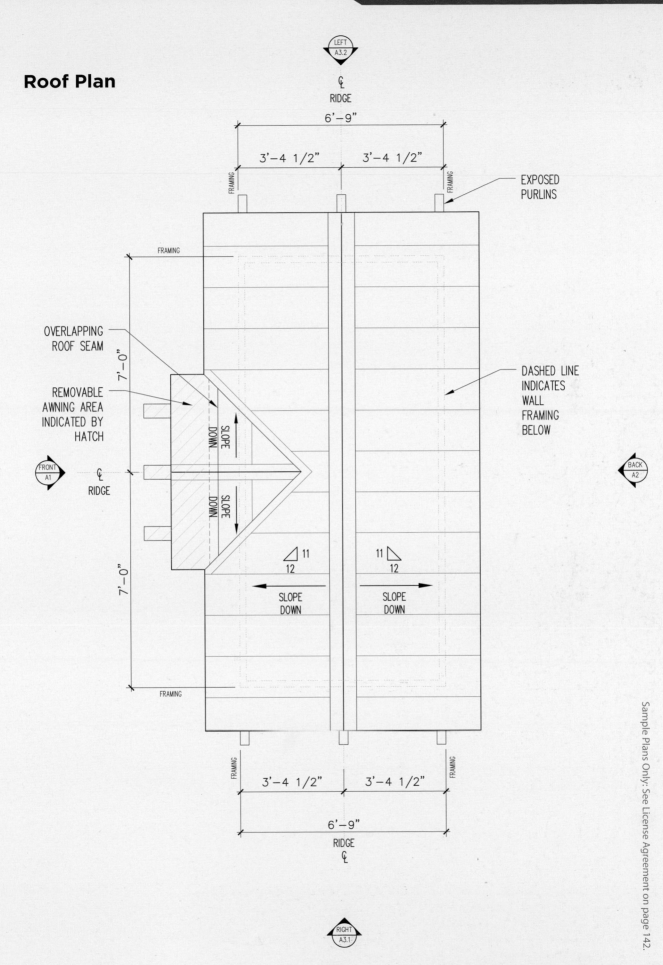

LEFT
A3.2

C̵
RIDGE

6'−9"

3'−4 1/2"   3'−4 1/2"

FRAMING   FRAMING

EXPOSED
PURLINS

FRAMING

OVERLAPPING
ROOF SEAM

DASHED LINE
INDICATES
WALL
FRAMING
BELOW

REMOVABLE
AWNING AREA
INDICATED BY
HATCH

7'−0"

SLOPE
DOWN

SLOPE
DOWN

FRONT
A1

C̵
RIDGE

BACK
A2

7'−0"

11
12

11
12

SLOPE
DOWN

SLOPE
DOWN

FRAMING

FRAMING

3'−4 1/2"   3'−4 1/2"

FRAMING

6'−9"

RIDGE
C̵

RIGHT
A3.1

Window Options-Front

T.O. RIDGE

3'-9 1/2"

LOFT LEVEL

11'-2"

6'-10 1/4"

MAIN FLOOR

B.O. FRAMING

6 1/4"

Window Options-Back

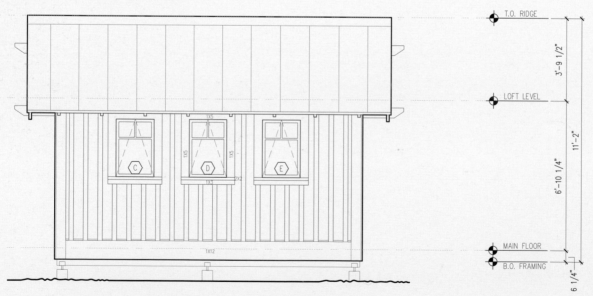

T.O. RIDGE

3'-9 1/2"

LOFT LEVEL

11'-2"

6'-10 1/4"

MAIN FLOOR

B.O. FRAMING

6 1/4"

Sample Plans Only: See License Agreement on page 142.

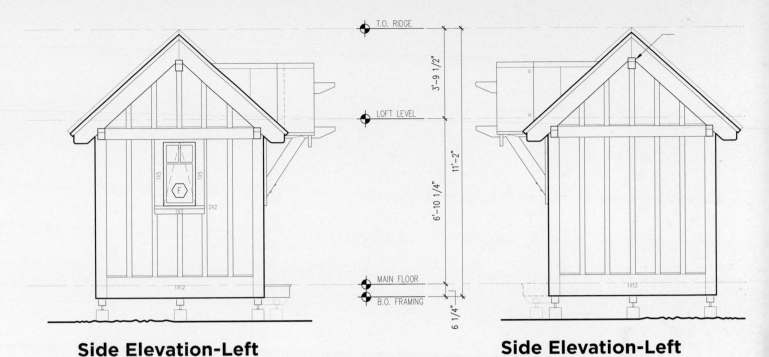

T.O. RIDGE

LOFT LEVEL

MAIN FLOOR

B.O. FRAMING

3'-9 1/2"

11'-2"

6'-10 1/4"

6 1/4"

Side Elevation-Left

Side Elevation-Left

Components for The Zinn :

WINDOW OPTIONS:

    A. MARVIN CLAD LOW-E AWNING WINDOW. 2-OVER-1 SDL.
       21" X 35 $\frac{5}{8}$" R.O.

    B. MARVIN CLAD LOW-E AWNING WINDOW. 2-OVER-1 SDL.
       21" X 35 $\frac{5}{8}$" R.O.

    C. (OPTIONAL) MARVIN CLAD LOW-E AWNING WINDOW. 2-OVER-1 SDL.
       21" X 31 $\frac{5}{8}$" R.O

    D. (OPTIONAL) MARVIN CLAD LOW-E AWNING WINDOW. 2-OVER-1 SDL.
       21" X 31 $\frac{5}{8}$" R.O

    E. (OPTIONAL) MARVIN CLAD LOW-E AWNING WINDOW. 2-OVER-1 SDL.
       21" X 31 $\frac{5}{8}$" R.O

    F. (OPTIONAL) MARVIN CLAD LOW-E AWNING WINDOW. 2-OVER-1 SDL.
       17" X 31 $\frac{5}{8}$" R.O

DOOR :

    A-1. FRONT DOOR ; CUSTOM. 2'-3$\frac{3}{4}$" x 6'-0"

Massive purlins, expansive eves and organic materials put
The Gifford squarely in the Craftsman tradition.

PART THREE:
TINY HOUSE PORTFOLIO

BY JAY SHAFER OF FOUR LIGHTS TINY HOUSE COMPANY

The Gifford

We have finished interior options and we've got shells. For folks interested in designing their own interior and overseeing the finish work inside but not dealing with the more structural concerns of framing and sheathing, a shell makes perfect sense. For those who'd rather stick to a tried-and-true layout, we offer the following furnished houses.

The Weller

The Beavan

The Zinn

The Marmara

The Marie Colvin

THE GIFFORD

112 SQUARE FEET
+ 48 SQUARE FOOT LOFT

The Gifford is the design of Jay Shafer's own house. It's a stunning 7' x 16' structure squarely rooted in the American Craftsman Style. It has been beefed up where beefing up was necessary for a sense of mass and fortification, and it has been pared down everywhere else. It has a standing seam, metal roof, cedar board-and-batten siding and a tiny integral porch that's good for staying dry as you perch or fumble for your keys. The interior is all knotty pine. The cathedral ceiling is 9' 8" tall at the peak. As a shell, it accommodates any of the components listed on the Compact Furnishings page and more.

Ironically, this little thing was inspired by the sizable Great Lodges of North America. When you enter it, you enter into a relatively narrow space that opens into a relatively huge space with a cathedral ceiling to increase the sense of mass and fortification.

The bathroom's interior is 21" x 53"; the great room is 96" x 75"; the kitchen is 53" x 46"; and the sleeping loft is just 75" W x 91 ¾" L x 33" H. Two skylights over the pillows make it feel much bigger. There's a 20 ½" x 57" desk/dining table, a stainless steel fireplace by Dickinson Marine and a couple of puffy chairs for entertaining.

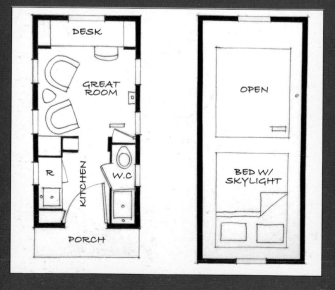

THE WELLER

115 SQUARE FEET
+ 48 SQUARE FOOT LOFT

People seem to love this one more than any other of Jay Shafer's tiniest home designs. Maybe it's because of the little bump out on the front—perfectly serving as a dining or reading nook.

Whatever the reason, this house employs the same American Craftsman principles as all of the Jay's newest tiny house designs— mass, volume and organic form predominate inside and out. The Weller embodies the same classical geometry, anthropometrics, and archetypal form Jay has used to create all of the Four Lights Houses. The Craftsman crusade put a high value on simplicity, natural materials and honest craftsmanship in the service of good design. Traditional Craftsman Bungalows, like the ones in this collection, are distinguished by their exposed structural elements, mass, broad eaves and by the movement's intention to make thoughtful design available to ordinary people.

The "furnished" house plans include a bathroom of 21" x 53"; a great room of 6' x 6' (average); a 54" x 46" kitchen and a sleeping loft of just 75" W x 96" L x 33" H. Like the Gifford, two skylights over the pillows make the loft feel much bigger. There's a dining nook and a stainless steel fireplace by Dickinson Marine. A twin-sized bed provides space for a (presumably) single occupant to sleep downstairs. A sleeping loft provides ample sleeping room for 2 guests (not to mention the fold-out sleeping chair in the great room for another one).

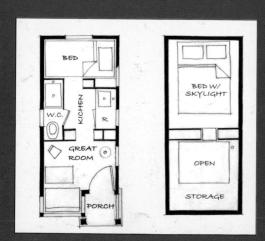

THE BEAVAN

**112 SQUARE FEET
+ 42 SQUARE FOOT LOFT**

The most notable distinction this house offers is the oversized, exposed truss above its integral porch. This shameless display of structural integrity, organic materials, and utility are derived from the Bungalow tradition that inspired the home. The more rustic elements of Craftsman style cabins and lodges are particularly evident.

The Beavan has a standing seam metal roof, cedar board and batten siding, and a tiny integral porch that's good for staying dry as you perch or fumble for your keys. The interior is all knotty pine. The cathedral ceiling is 9' 8" tall at the peak. As a shell, it accommodates any of the components listed on the Compact Furnishings page and more.

The bathroom's interior is 21" x 53"; the great room is 6' 3" x 5' 8"; the kitchen is 6' 3" x 4' 4"; and the sleeping loft is just 75" W x 76" L x 33" H. Two skylights over the pillows make it feel much bigger. A Dickinson Marine fireplace keeps the place warm and cozy.

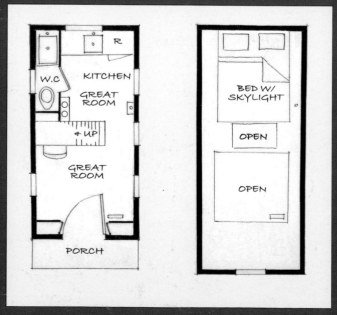

THE ZINN

98 SQUARE FEET
+ 42 SQUARE FOOT LOFT

At 14' x 7', this beautiful little house is our smallest, most affordable, and easiest to build. Two beefy purlins flanking the front door support a gable awning on the structure's long side. A sense of mass and fortification inside make this one a favorite amongst fans of the traditional Craftsman Style.

The Zinn has a standing seam metal roof and can be clad in clapboard or board and batten siding. The interior is all knotty pine. The cathedral ceiling is 9' 8" tall at the peak. As a shell, it accommodates any of the components listed on the Compact Furnishings page and more.

The bathroom's interior is 21" x 53". The great room is 96" x 83" and the sleeping loft is just 75" W x 76" L x 33" H. A skylight over the head of the bed makes it feel much bigger. There's a stainless steel fireplace by Dickinson Marine, an additional foldout bed downstairs, and lots of storage.

THE MARMARA

262 SQUARE FEET + 150 SQUARE FEET OF LOFT SPACE

Small house living doesn't necessarily entail living in a house the size of a Ford Ranger. In fact, I don't think most lives would fit into a single parking space. In its original and, I believe, its truest form, the Small House Movement was created not so much as a showcase for living "'tinier than thou,' but rather people making their own choices toward simpler and smaller living however they feel best fits their life." —Greg Johnson, co-founder and president of the Small House Society, 2002.

The Marmara is considerably larger than Four Lights' tiniest houses. At 262 square feet downstairs and an additional 150 square feet up in the loft, it's nearly three times the size of the smallest houses.

Among other features, the Marmara allows for the finished design to contain a full-sized bed downstairs, along with a kitchen of more than 200 cubic feet of storage, a 30" x 78" bathroom, a 9' 6" x 10' great room and more than 70 square feet of storage. There are two sleeping/storage lofts to accommodate four guests comfortably and/or a lot of surplus storage. The little gas fireplace is by Jotul.

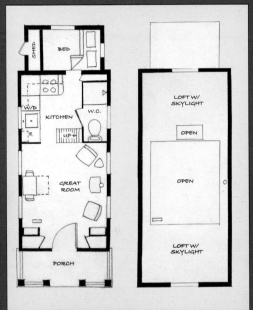

THE MARIE COLVIN

288 SQUARE FEET
+ 130 SQUARE FEET OF LOFT SPACE

One of my highly anticipated larger house designs, The Marie Colvin is now available as both a shell and a furnished plan. This house boasts a beautiful bump-out dining nook/study, a downstairs bedroom, two lofts, a kitchen with ample storage, a 2' 6" x 6' 6" bathroom, a 9' 6" x 10' great room and more than 70 square feet of storage. The furnished plan sets come with a main floor plan, a loft floor plan, an electrical plan, trailer specifications with an alternate pier foundation plan, pertinent detail elevations and all of the integral component plans, including the blueprints for furniture designed specifically to fit in a tiny house.

NAPOLEON COMPLEX

My friends Yohan Morgan and Mark Sowers and I have been talking with Sonoma County's zoning department about building a tiny house village. The officials seem to love this idea as much as we do, so we've started investigating some of the details involved and taking concrete steps to make it all happen.

In many ways, tiny houses work best in concert with other tiny houses and shared amenities. This is a dream long-shared by many, including myself. The place will be zoned as an R.V. park, but will look and feel more like the concept drawings I'm presenting to the left. I've used the same design principles that go into each of my tiny house designs to create an environment that feels contained but not confining—vibrant but not at all crowded.

All Four Lights Houses can be mounted on footings or on wheels.

PART FOUR:

HOW TO BUILD A TINY HOUSE

BY THE EDITORS OF SKILLS INSTITUTE PRESS

CLEARING THE BUILDING SITE

Before you can building in your backyard or anywhere else, you will need to prepare the site, mostly by removing any vegetation, boulders, and small trees that are in your way. On rough sites, this can be a formidable task but for a small building in your backyard it's more likely to be quite straightforward. When the area has been cleared you can begin construction by laying whatever type of foundation suits the site and the structure you plan to build.

CLEARING VEGETATION

Cut bushes down to ground level with a pair of pruning shears, and dig the roots up with a shovel the same way you would those of a small tree (page 77). Clear tall grass and vines with a gas-powered trimmer; or use a scythe or a hand sickle, always holding your free hand away from the blade.

REMOVING TREES

Felling large, mature trees is a relatively complex operation, but a chain saw can put the job within anyone's reach (page 75). Until you are experienced at working with a power saw, however, restrict your efforts to trunks whose diameter is less than the length of the saw blade. It is easier to fell a tree in the direction of its natural lean, but this may not always be possible. You can direct a tree away from its natural lean using wedges and a tapered hinge cut in the trunk.

REMOVING ROCKS

For stones that are too large for you to budge, wrap rope or a chain around it and use a comealong (page 76). Or, split them into smaller pieces that can be moved more easily: Fit a drill with a masonry bit and bore holes in the rocks, then drive in steel wedges with a sledgehammer until the rocks break apart.

SAFETY TIPS

Put on a hard hat, goggles or a face shield, hearing protection, Kevlar chaps, work gloves, and steel-toed boots when working with a chain saw.

CAUTION

Before you start cutting any tree, plan an escape route—ideally at about a 45-degree angle from the proposed direction of the fall—and remove all obstacles from the path.

CHAIN-SAW SAFETY GEAR

If you are clearing away a large number of trees with a chain saw, it is essential to wear special safety clothing. Leg coverings, or chaps, as well as the boots and gloves, are lined with a protective material such as Kevlar that is reinforced to resist being cut through. The helmet incorporates ear protection and a face shield.

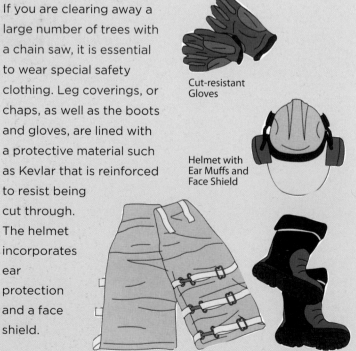

Cut-resistant Gloves

Helmet with Ear Muffs and Face Shield

Protective Chaps

Safety Boots

TOOLS
- Chain saw
- Sledgehammer
- Wooden wedges

A LIGHTWEIGHT CHAIN SAW

In addition to severing tree trunks and branches, a lightweight chain saw can double as an all-purpose wood-cutting tool.

A lightweight saw can weigh about 10 pounds, making it easy to handle.

THE SAFE WAY TO FELL A TREE

1. CUTTING A NOTCH IN THE TRUNK.

On the side of the tree that faces the direction of its natural lean, hold a chain saw with the blade angled at 45 degrees to the trunk.

Turn on the engine, let it come to full throttle, and make an angled cut about one-third of the way through the trunk. Pull the blade from the cut.

Holding the blade horizontally at the bottom of the angled cut, saw to the end of the cut *(right)*. Retract the blade and push the wedge-shaped piece from the notch.

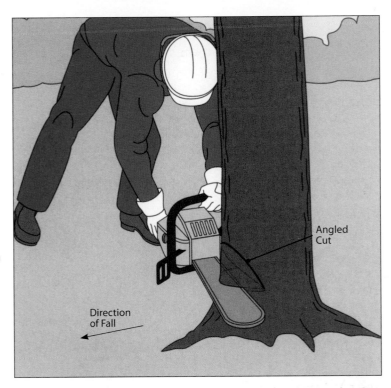

Angled Cut

Direction of Fall

2. MAKING THE FELLING CUT.

On the side of the trunk opposite the notch, start a horizontal cut 2 inches above the bottom of the notch *(right)*.

Stop cutting when the blade is 2 to 3 inches from the back of the notch, creating a hinge *(below)*. The trunk will pivot on the hinge, and the tree should fall. If not, drive in wedges.

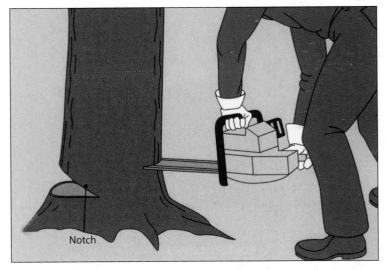

Notch

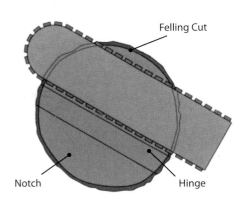

Felling Cut

Notch

Hinge

REMOVING LOGS, STUMPS, AND ROOTS

TOOLS
- Heavy-duty chains
- Hook for chain
- Comealong
- Flat spade

Once large trees are cut down, you can maneuver the logs around your building site with a hand-operated comealong. Rather than chopping down small trees and then getting rid of the roots, you can uproot them (*page 77*), then either dispose of them or replant them somewhere else on the site.

TRANSPLANTING TREES

If you opt for transplanting, keep in mind that trees taller than 10 feet with trunks that are greater than 3 inches thick will be unwieldy to move and will be less likely to survive when replanted. A tree's chances are greatest if you transplant in a period of low growth activity—in spring before leaves appear, or in autumn after they fall.

MOVING LOGS

The comealong, a tool with a ratchet mechanism and a lever that is moved back and forth to reel in a cable, gives you the mechanical advantage needed to clear out heavy logs by hand (*below*).

REMOVING STUMPS

For trees that were already cut down, uproot small stumps the same way you would a small tree; larger ones can be ground down to below grade using a rented stump grinder (*page 77*). For very large stumps, it's best to hire a professional to remove them.

SAFETY TIPS
Wear steel-toed safety boots when moving logs.

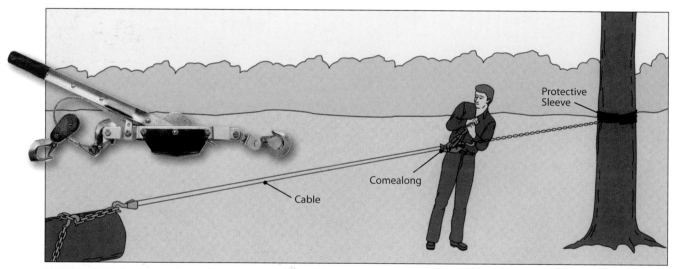

Protective Sleeve

Comealong

Cable

DRAGGING A LOG WITH A COMEALONG

Wrap a heavy-duty chain with a hook around the log, about 2 feet from the end, using the hook to hold the chain in place.

Fasten a second chain, without a hook, around the trunk of a tree in the direction you want to pull the log. Unless you will be cutting down this tree, protect the bark with a sleeve, such as a bicycle inner tube.

Hook the extendable cable of a comealong (*photograph*) to the chain on the log, and hook the stationary end to the chain around the tree.

Draw the log toward the tree by moving the handle on the comealong back and forth (*above*).

Release the tension mechanism on the comealong, remove the chain from the tree, attach it to another tree further along, and repeat the process as many times as necessary to move the log off the building site.

DIGGING OUT SMALL TREES OR STUMPS

REMOVING THE ROOTBALL

Using a flat spade with a sharp blade, slice through the roots in a 30- to 36-inch-wide circle around the trunk. Push the blade into the ground at about a 30-degree angle toward the trunk to taper the root ball for easy removal *(right)*.

Dig a 24- to 30-inch-deep access trench around the rootball.

Sever the taproot—the root section that heads straight down into the ground—and any other uncut roots under the tree with the spade. With a helper, lift out the tree and rootball.

Taproot   Rootball

A PORTABLE STUMP GRINDER

An alternative to the labor-intensive process of chopping or digging up stumps is to rent a stump grinder. This gas-powered machine has an angled blade that shaves a stump down to ground level quickly and easily. On some models, the handlebars can be attached to a holder at one end of the tool, as shown here, or to a longer holder at the other end, to allow the cutter to reach stumps near obstructions. A tough rubber flap deflects chips away from the operator, but be sure to wear goggles when you are running the machine.

A FOUNDATION ON POLES

From a distance, a shed resting on wooden poles may look shaky and fragile. In reality, such a foundation can provide decades of stalwart support and withstand storms and floods.

SITE SUITABILITY

Pole platforms cannot be used everywhere. In some localities, building codes require continuous-wall foundations. Walls are also recommended in earthquake-prone regions, cold climates, and on building sites with insecure soil— such as sand or soft clay—or a slope greater than 1 in 10—1 foot of rise for every 10 horizontal feet. The techniques on these pages are designed only for fairly level sites with stable soil.

LUMBER AND CONCRETE

Buy pressure-treated poles that are reasonably straight and uniform in diameter, and get enough to space them about 8 feet apart. For a level site, they need to be long enough to extend 1½ to 3 feet above ground level and at least 4 feet below it, or at least 6 inches below the frost line if it is deeper than 4 feet. Where the ground slopes gently, buy poles that are 1 foot longer. For the beams, obtain pressure-treated lumber long enough to span the rows of poles.

To anchor poles in their holes (*page 79, Step 2*), you will need concrete or a wet mixture of 1 part Portland cement to 5 parts clean soil, free of roots, leaves, and other organic matter. Prepare this mixture by combining the dry ingredients, then adding slightly less water than you would for concrete—the amount of water will vary depending on the soil.

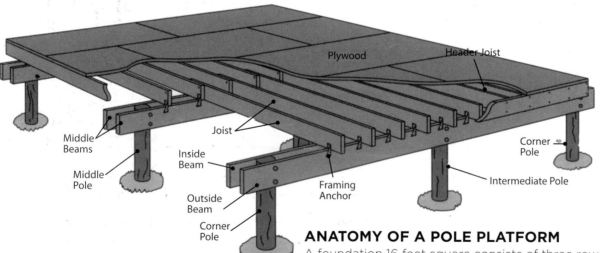

Middle Beams

Middle Pole

Joist

Inside Beam

Outside Beam

Corner Pole

Framing Anchor

Plywood

Header Joist

Corner Pole

Intermediate Pole

ANATOMY OF A POLE PLATFORM

A foundation 16 feet square consists of three rows of pressure-treated poles sunk into the ground at 8-foot intervals. Each pole is firmly anchored in a jacket of concrete or soil-cement mixture; the tops of the poles are sandwiched between 2-by-10 pressure-treated beams, fastened in place with ½-inch carriage bolts, washers, and nuts. The 2-by-6 pressure-treated floor joists, which span from the outside beams to the middle beams, are fastened to the beams with framing anchors. They are also nailed to a header joist at each end of the foundation. The outer joists are placed to coincide with the eventual location of the cabin's walls. Sheets of plywood nailed across the joists can serve as a subfloor or as a finish floor.

PUTTING UP A POLE PLATFORM

1. DIGGING THE HOLES.

Lay out the site as you would for a block wall, marking the location of the poles in relation to the walls.

Rent a power auger to dig each posthole to a depth of 4 feet or at least 6 inches below the frost line, whichever is deeper. You can use a one-man power auger *(photograph)*, but a two-man version *(right)* is more powerful and easier to handle.

With a spade and a clamshell post-hole digger, widen the holes to 16 to 18 inches in diameter.

Set all the poles in their holes.

On a gently sloping site—one with a rise of 1 in 10 or less—you will need to dig the postholes deeper and larger than those on a level site; consult local building codes or a building professional.

TOOLS
- Maul
- Hammer
- Tape measure (50-foot)
- Plumb bob
- Power auger
- Garden spade
- Posthole digger
- Carpenter's level
- Line level
- 2 x 4 tamper
- Bucksaw
- Electric drill with auger bit (½")
- Wrench
- Circular saw

MATERIALS
- 1 x 2s, 1 x 6s
- 2 x 4s, 2 x 8s
- Pressure-treated poles (6"–8" thick)
- Pressure-treated 2 x 6s, 2 x 10s
- Exterior-grade plywood (¾")
- Ring-shank nails (2")
- Galvanized common nails (2½", 3")
- Multipurpose framing anchors and nails
- Carriage bolts (½"), washers, and nuts
- Powdered chalk
- Concrete mix or Portland cement and clean soil

2. SETTING THE POLES.

Plumb the corner poles with a level and, while a helper holds them straight, brace them with 1-by-2s nailed to stakes.

Measure down from the top of one corner pole the width of a beam plus 3 inches, and make a mark there. Drive a nail at the mark.

Stretch a string fitted with a line level from the nail to the other corner post, and mark the second corner post at the height of the level string. Drive a nail there and tie the string to it.

Align the middle pole with the string, then plumb and brace it *(above)*. Mark the point where the string touches the pole.

Prepare enough concrete or cement-soil mixture to fill in around the poles and shovel it into each hole, overfilling it slightly. Tamp the mixture with a 2-by-4, sloping the top downward from the pole to the ground.

Repeat the process on the other rows of poles, then remove the strings and nails and let the concrete cure for a day.

WORKING WITH CONCRETE IN THE WILDERNESS.

To save you the trouble of having to mix separate ingredients for concrete—Portland cement, sand, and gravel—get the cement and sand premixed. Protect the dry ingredients by placing the bags on wooden pallets and covering them with plastic sheets or tarpaulins.

To clean up your tools after a day's work without the luxury of running water, keep a 6-gallon bucket of water on hand, and when you're finished with a tool, place it in the bucket. Replace the water as necessary, but use it to clean out the wheelbarrow before discarding it.

3. STARTING THE DAPS.

To enable the beams to sit squarely against the poles, you'll need to cut a notch, called a dap, on both sides of each pole near the top. With a buck-saw or pruning saw, first make a series of horizontal cuts 1½ inches wide and ⅛ to ¼ inch deep on one side of the pole (right). Work from the top of the pole to the mark you made in Step 2.

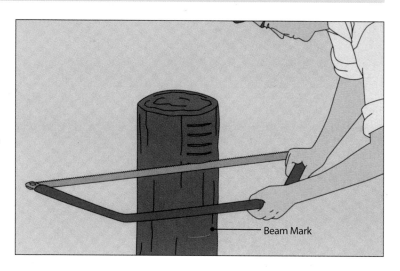
Beam Mark

4. FINISHING THE DAPS.

Place the saw on top of the pole and align the blade with the ends of the horizontal cuts on one side, then saw down through the cuts from the top of the pole to the beam mark (left).

Cut daps on the same side of the remaining poles.

Dap

5. LOCATING THE OUTSIDE BEAMS.

With a helper, set a beam against the outside of one row of poles so the bottom edge sits squarely in the daps in the posts.

Holding the beam level, temporarily fasten it to each pole with a 3-inch common nail *(left)*.

Nail a beam to the outsides of each remaining row of poles in the same way.

Cut the tops of the poles flush with the tops of the beams.

6. POSITIONING THE INSIDE BEAMS.

With a helper, run a string across a row of poles on the side opposite the beam *(above)*.

Line up the string with the edge of the pole that is smallest in diameter *(inset)*.

Mark the tops of the larger poles at the string line, and cut a dap *(page 80, Steps 3 and 4)* at each mark.

Temporarily nail beams to the inside of the poles as described above.

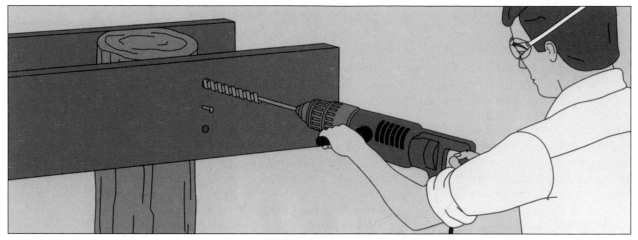

7. BOLTING THE BEAMS TO THE POLES.

Measure and mark a point one-third of the way from the top and bottom of each beam.

Install a ½-inch auger bit in an electric drill and bore a hole through the beams and pole at each mark *(above)*.

Insert a ½-inch carriage bolt about 1 inch longer than the combined thickness of the beams and pole into each hole.

Tighten washers and nuts onto the bolts.

As wood tends to shrink over time, check the nuts for tightness several weeks after the foundation is completed, and tighten them as necessary.

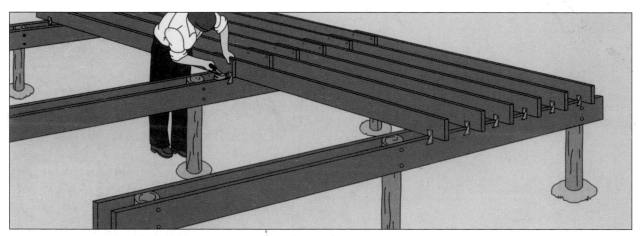

8. ATTACHING THE FLOOR JOISTS.

Set the joists across the beams at 16-inch intervals, letting them extend beyond the outside beams by a foot and overlap at the center beams by a foot.

With 3-inch common nails, fasten together the joists that overlap at the center beams.

Fasten the joists to the beams with multipurpose framing anchors and the nails recommended by the manufacturer of the anchors *(above)*.

Nail header joists across the outside ends of the floor joists, and fasten them to the end of each joist with 2½-inch common nails.

Lay a subfloor across the joists *(page 92)*.

MASONRY PIERS FOR STRONGER SUPPORTS

Piers make a more durable foundation than wooden poles, and are almost as easy to put up. You can make them in three different ways: by pouring concrete into cylindrical fiber forms; by stacking and mortaring masonry-block piers and filling the cores of the blocks with concrete; or by setting precast piers of solid concrete.

DEALING WITH A SLOPE

As with pole platforms, piers can be used on gently sloping sites, provided the piers and their footing holes are deeper and wider than on a level site; consult a building professional. But if the slope is greater than 1 in 10—1 foot of rise in every 10 horizontal feet—you will have to build a continuous-wall foundation.

FOOTINGS

All three types of piers rest on footings—solid concrete bases that are wide and thick enough to support the structures above them. In general, a footing should be as thick as the width of a pier, and twice as wide—a pier 8 inches wide, for example, would require a footing 8 inches thick and 16 inches wide. Dig the holes so the bottom of the footing is 1 foot below ground, or 6 inches below the frost line, whichever is deeper.

CAST CYLINDERS

Fiber tubes 8 inches in diameter and 10 feet long make quick work of casting cylindrical concrete piers (page 84); store them upright and keep them perfectly dry until they are filled. Cylindrical piers can be built to any height, making it easy to set the tops of the piers to the same level.

MASONRY BLOCKS

These blocks come in a wide range of sizes; single-core, 8- by-12- by- 12-inch blocks make particularly sturdy piers (page 86, top). Level the footings for block piers with a water level in the same way you level forms (page 84, Step 3), but mark the height on the reinforcing bars (rebars), then measure down from the marks to set the height of the concrete for the footings.

PRECAST PIERS

Although simple to install, these piers (page 86, bottom) are heavy and awkward to move and set into position. To level their footings, drive stakes into the footing holes, mark stakes with a water level as you would for concrete forms (page 84), pour concrete up to the marks, and remove the stakes before the concrete begins to harden. Because they generally come no more than 18 inches high, they are used mainly on level sites that have a shallow frost line.

TOOLS	MATERIALS
■ Maul	■ 1 x 2s, 1 x 6s, 2 x 4s
■ Hammer	■ Pressure-treated lumber (2 x 10 or 2 x 12)
■ Tape measure (50-foot)	■ Galvanized common nails (3")
■ Plumb bob	■ Powdered chalk
■ Power auger	■ Rebar (½")
■ Garden spade	■ Concrete mix
■ Posthole digger	■ Fiber forms
■ Rebar cutter	■ Beam anchors
■ Tamper	■ Polyethylene sheeting (6-mil)
■ Carpenter's level	■ Galvanized washers
■ Water level	■ Concrete blocks
■ Hacksaw	■ Precast piers
■ Mason's trowel	■ Mortar
	■ Grout

CASTING CONCRETE

1. CASTING THE FOOTINGS.

Locate and dig the footing-and-pier holes as for a pole platform *(page 79, Step 1)*, excavating each hole 16 inches wide to the required depth.

At the center of each hole, drive a length of ½ inch rebar into the ground until the top of the rod is about 6 inches lower than the planned height of the pier above ground *(right)*.

Fill the first 8 inches of the holes with concrete, creating footings. Allow the concrete to cure for at least one day.

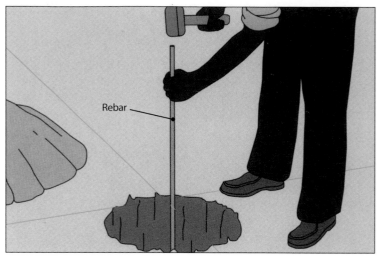

Rebar

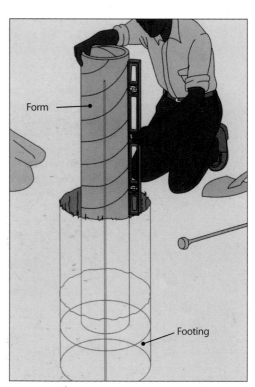

Form

Footing

2. POSITIONING THE FORMS.

Slide a form over each rebar so it rests on the footing.

Fill the hole around the form with earth, tamping it down firmly. After every 6 inches of fill, check that the form is vertical with a carpenter's level *(above)*.

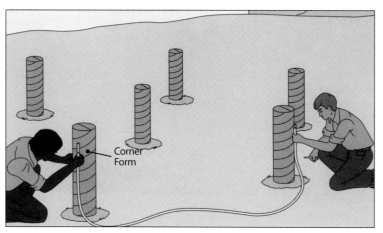

Corner Form

3. LEVELING THE FORMS.

Mark the planned height of the piers on a corner form.

Have a helper hold one end of a water level or a transparent hose filled almost completely with water at the height of the mark on the corner form.

Hold the other end against the next form in the row *(above)* and mark a line at the level of the water.

Repeat the process to mark each form.

Cut the forms at the marked heights with a hacksaw.

4. EMBEDDING THE ANCHORS IN CONCRETE.

With a helper and a string, go from form to form to align and mark the position of a beam anchor on the front and back of each form, ensuring that each beam—3 inches wide for doubled 2-by-10s or 2-by-12s, or 4½ inches for a triple beam—will be centered on the pier.

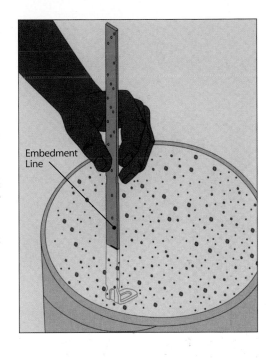

Mix enough concrete to fill the forms, then shovel it into each form in the row, using a length of rebar to pack the concrete down with every foot you add.

As you fill each form, level the concrete off with the top of the form using a 2-by-4, then following the marks on the form, push an anchor that is as long as the width of the beams to be installed *(Step 5)* into the concrete down to the embedment line marked on it.

Embed anchors in concrete in the remaining forms in the same way.

Double-check the alignment of the anchors with the string, adjusting them to line up as needed.

Allow the concrete to cure for five to seven days.

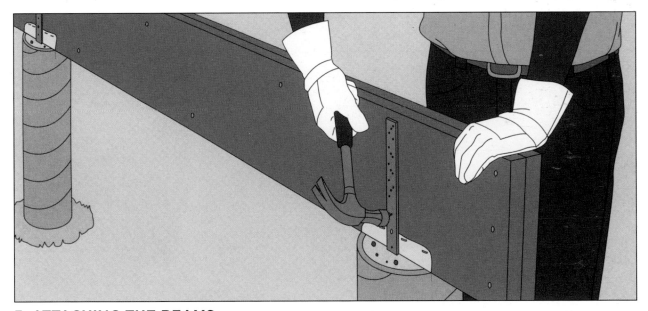

5. ATTACHING THE BEAMS.

Make a beam for each row of piers: For a prefab cabin *(pages 122-129)*, nail pairs of 2-by-10s or 2-by-12s together with 3-inch galvanized common nails. Drive three nails in a row about 1 inch from each end and stagger nails along both edges at 10-inch intervals. For an A-frame *(page 106)*, make triple beams.

For a vapor barrier, set asphalt shingles on the piers, or cut 6-mil polyethylene sheeting into pieces to wrap around the bottom of the beam at each pier, and staple the pieces to the beam.

Set the beam into its anchor, then check whether it is level. If not, shim the low end by placing galvanized washers between the beam and pier.

Fasten the beam to each anchor by nailing into each hole *(above)*.

Fasten joists to the beams as for a pole foundation *(page 82, Step 8)*, then lay a subfloor across the joists *(page 92)*.

BLOCK AND PRECAST PIERS

CONCRETE-BLOCK PIERS

Cast a footing for each pier as for concrete piers *(page 84, Step 1)*, but level the footings by marking the rebars with a water level as for concrete forms *(page 84)*.

To keep the heights of the piers consistent, make a story pole: On a piece of lumber, mark lines at intervals equal to the height of a block plus a ⅜-inch mortar joint.

Trowel a bed of mortar on the footing and lay a concrete block on the mortar, centering the block around the rebar.

Add blocks and mortar to build up the pier, checking each course for level and plumb with a carpenter's level *(right)*, and for height with the story pole.

Build each remaining pier in the same way, running a string between adjacent piers to keep them all consistent and in alignment.

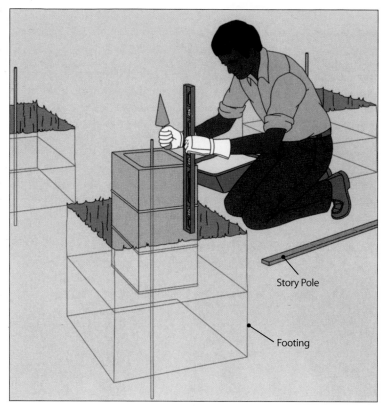

Story Pole

Footing

Fill the cores of the piers with grout—concrete thinned with water so it can be poured—then embed concrete anchors in the piers and attach beams as for concrete piers *(page 85, Steps 4 and 5)*.

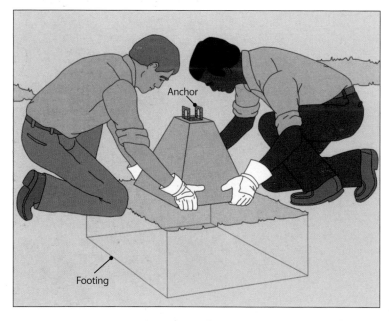

Anchor

Footing

PRECAST-CONCRETE PIERS

Cast a footing for each pier as for concrete piers *(page 84, Step 1)*, but proceed immediately, before the concrete cures.

With a helper, press a precast pier into the wet concrete *(left)*.

With a carpenter's level, ensure that the pier is level.

Position each remaining pier in the same way, running a string between adjacent ones to keep them aligned and level.

Install vapor barriers and attach beams to the piers' built-in anchors as you would for concrete piers *(page 85, Step 5)*, nailing exterior-grade plywood spacers at 24-inch intervals between the boards making up the beam, if necessary, to ensure the beam sits snugly in the anchors.

GAZEBO

The gazebo is an open post-and-beam structure, usually with five, six, or eight sides and a peaked roof. The version shown here is six-sided, and can be built up to 12 feet in diameter—a larger gazebo requires collar ties to connect opposing rafters; the collar ties are fastened to the bottom end of the rafters. A gazebo can be left open or covered with woven reed or bamboo, with fiberglass or aluminum screening, or with lattice.

A gazebo's foundation can often be as simple as concrete blocks or 6-by-6 wooden blocks set under the corner of the platform. If the site is uneven, embed the blocks in the earth. Before beginning, always check local building codes; some may require a more substantial footing.

JOINING GAZEBO RAFTERS

Even if gazebo rafters are cut accurately to length and angle, assembling them can be a juggling act. Commercial roof peak rafter ties (*below*) take much of the guesswork out of the job by allowing the ends of the rafters to be sawn square. The ties are flexible enough to accommodate different pitch roofs.

Gazebo connectors are also available to fasten rafters to crossbeams; others are designed to join the perimeter boards at the correct angle without requiring miter cuts.

ANATOMY OF A HEXAGONAL GAZEBO

Six 4-by-4 posts toenailed to a wood platform and secured to the beam-and-rafter unit that forms the roof provide the uprights of this post-and-beam structure. The gazebo platform consists of perimeter boards, joists, and decking—all made from 2-by-6s. Six crossbeams, five handrails (all 2-by-4s), and six plywood arches give the structure lateral rigidity. The 2-by-6 roof rafters are nailed at their bases to the crossbeams and attached at their peaks to 2-by-4 spacers. The entire structure rests on concrete blocks.

CUTTING PARTS FOR DIFFERENT-SHAPED GAZEBOS

The lengths of the perimeter boards and crossbeams are determined by the number of sides of the gazebo, and by its overall size. Base your calculations on a circle whose area is about equal to the floor area of the gazebo you plan to build. If your gazebo will be hexagonal, its sides must be the same length as the circle's radius; for a pentagon, multiply the radius by 1.25; for an octagon, multiply the radius by .75. Cut the perimeter boards to length and miter their ends to an angle of 30 degrees for a hexagon, 36 degrees for a pentagon, or 22½ degrees for an octagon. Cut the spacers (the boards that separate the rafters) the same way.

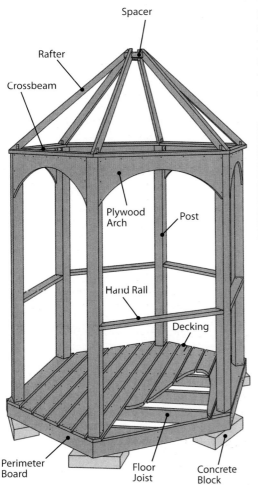

Spacer

Rafter

Crossbeam

Plywood Arch

Post

Hand Rail

Decking

Perimeter Board

Floor Joist

Concrete Block

POST-AND-BEAM: A CLASSIC METHOD REVIVED

Post-and-beam structures are an elegant complement to outdoor living. Built with pressure-treated wood and left without sheathing, the post-and-beam framework can be used as an arbor or a trellis; roofed and sheathed with openwork materials, it becomes a garden shelter. With weatherproof siding and roofing, the structure can be a workshop, shed, or studio.

FOUNDATIONS

For an open-roofed structure, a simple concrete slab or set of precast concrete piers is adequate foundation *(page 86)*. A closed-roofed structure, particularly one that must bear the weight of snow, requires a turned-down slab or concrete piers with footings set below the frost line. The latter is similar to the footings for the brick wall except the blocks are built at each post location rather than along the whole outline.

THE POSTS AND BEAMS

The size of the posts for an unroofed structure is determined by the building's width. Long, narrow structures are easier to build; if the width is less than 8 feet, 4-by-4 redwood or pressure-treated posts suffice. If the structure is wider than 8 feet but less than 12 feet, use 4-by-6 posts. Determining the size of posts for a roofed post-and-beam structure requires more precise calculations and varies from area to area. Consult your local building code.

The size of the beams is determined by the span between posts. The width in inches of a 4-inch beam should equal its span in feet. Thus, a 4-by-6 beam can span distances up to 6 feet, a 4-by-8 up to 8 feet, and so on.

CHOOSING RAFTERS

Rafters to bridge the beams can be spaced as far apart as 48 inches in an unroofed structure; use the table *at right* to determine the spacing and lengths of rafters for an open roof. If you plan to roof the structure, the rafters should be set no more than 16 inches apart. Use 2-by-4s for a structure up to 5 feet wide, 2-by-6s for up to 9 feet, 2-by-8s for up to 11 feet, and 2-by-10s for up to 14 feet.

Rafter Sizes for an Open Roof

Spacing	Maximum Rafter Length		
	8 ft.	10 ft.	12 ft.
16 in.	2 x 4	2 x 6	2 x 6
32 in.	2 x 6	2 x 6	2 x 8
48 in.	2 x 6	2 x 6	2 x 8

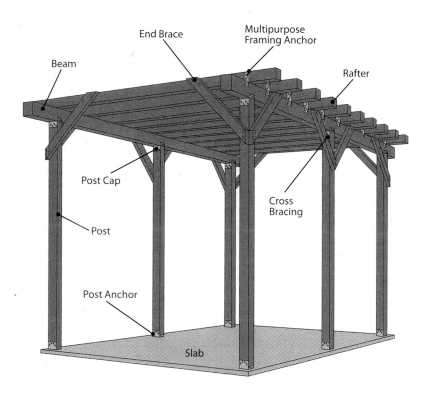

ANATOMY OF A POST-AND-BEAM STRUCTURE

Metal connectors hold together the basic post-and-beam framework. The posts are attached to post anchors fastened to a concrete slab *(above)* or to precast concrete piers *(page 86)*. At the tops of the posts, metal post caps secure the beams. Rafters are attached to beams with metal framing anchors. The beam ends overhang the posts below them, and the rafters overhang the beams. Diagonal 2-by-4 cross braces are attached with lag screws.

TOOLS
- Tape measure
- Carpenter's level
- Chalk line
- Hammer
- Maul
- Wrench
- Circular saw
- Electric drill
- ¾" masonry bit

MATERIALS
- 4-by posts
- 4-by beams
- 2-by rafters
- 2x4 braces
- Wooden stakes
- Common nails (2½")
- Lag screws (⅜"x3"; ½"x3½") and washers Post anchors and post caps Framing anchors
- Framing-anchor nails
- (1½", 2½", 3½") Lead shield

SAFETY TIPS
Wear goggles when hammering and drilling, and hard hat when working with materials overhead. Put on gloves when handling pressure-treated lumber; add a dust mask when cutting it.

ERECTING POSTS

1. SETTING THE POST ANCHORS.

The U-shaped anchors are bolted to the concrete slab with an offset washer that permits post positions to be shifted slightly for alignment.

Snap chalk lines 2 inches in from each side of the slab.

Place anchors and washers at each post position and mark the location for the lead shield.

Drill a ¾-inch hole 4 inches deep at each mark with a masonry bit. Drop a ¾-inch lead shield into the hole.

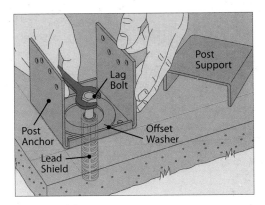

Place the post anchor and washer over the hole, then tighten a ½-inch lag screw into the shield until it is snug but the anchor can still be shifted.

Set a post support inside each anchor.

2. RAISING THE POSTS.

Install post caps on the top end of the posts with 3½-inch framing-anchor nails. Place a post onto the post anchor.

Have a helper hold the post plumb, checking with a carpenter's level on two adjacent sides.

Secure the bottom of the post to the anchor *(left)*.

Align the outside post edges with the building lines and tighten the lag screw *(inset)*. Repeat for all the other posts.

3. PLUMBING AND BRACING THE CORNERS.

While a helper holds the corner post plumb—checking with a level—brace the post with 2-by-4s nailed to stakes and to the post at least 20 inches from the top.

Repeat for each corner.

RAISING BEAMS

1. ATTACHING THE BEAMS.

Mark the tops of the beams for rafters, spacing them as desired; refer to the table on page 88 for maximum spacings and spans. Make the first mark to position the outside edge of an end rafter flush with the outside edge of a corner post.

Set each beam in the post caps atop a row of posts, marked-side up, aligning the outermost marks with the outside edges of the corner posts.

Have a helper hold the beam steady while you nail the corner post-cap flanges to the beam with 3½-inch nails designed for connectors.

Plumb the intermediate posts with a level, then nail them to the post-cap flanges (87).

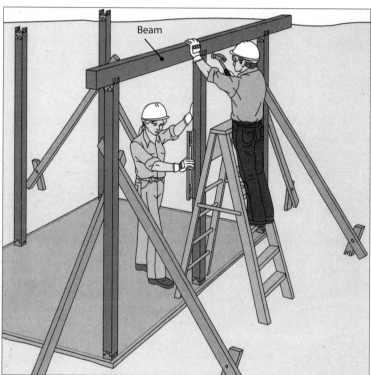

Beam

ALTERNATIVE WAYS TO ATTACH POST TO BEAMS

Galvanized metal connectors are a strong, utilitarian, and relatively foolproof way to hold the beams to the posts. But there are more attractive solutions, including the three shown at right. The half-lap is the strongest joint, especially with the addition of lag screws. The double beam works by bolting two beams to both sides of the post. The decorative cleat partially conceals a metal post cap connector.

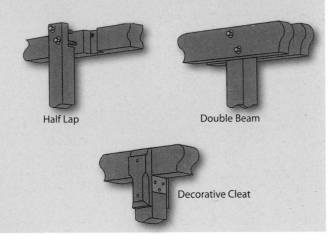

Half Lap   Double Beam

Decorative Cleat

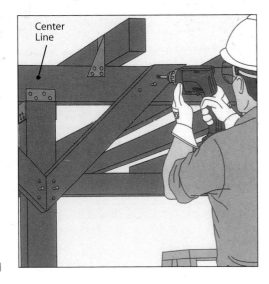

Rafter

12"

2. PUTTING UP RAFTERS.

Measure and cut the rafters following the table on page 88, adding 24 inches to the total length to give a ½-inch overhang on each side.

Nail a framing anchor to the top of one beam on one side of an end-rafter mark with 2½-inch connector nails.

Nail another anchor on the top of the opposite beam, on one side of the mark.

Make a mark on the side of a rafter 12 inches in from each end, set the rafter against the anchors, and nail it in place with 1½-inch nails (left).

Attach the remaining rafters the same way.

3. MOUNTING THE BRACES.

The 2-by-4 braces can be cut ahead of time. For most applications cut them at a 45-degree angle at each end and 26 inches in length along their longest edge.

Center Line

Tack the braces in position so one end is flush with the top of the beam and the other is aligned with the center line of the post. (For the end post align the lower end of the brace with the outside edge of the post.)

Drill a 5-inch-diameter pilot hole through the brace and into the beam or post. Secure the braces with ⅜-by-3-inch lag screws and washers, driving the screws in with a socket wrench.

Attach the end braces similarly, but position the higher end flush with the top of the rafter, as shown on page 90. This will mean cutting longer pieces than the standard cross braces.

Remove the temporary nails and bracing.

WOODEN FLOORS FOR COMFORT

Some structures—A-frames, tree houses, and gazebos—depend on floors for support. Others do not need floors because they rest on a concrete slab or below-ground footings. But you can cover bare ground with gravel or sand. To provide a dry and ventilated surface for walking or for storage, a wood floor may be desirable.

Two Types of Floor: For a permanent floor, build an understructure as shown. For a removable floor, build portable deck modules, called duckboards, which rest on the ground or on a slab.

Make the deck surface from pressure-treated 2-by-4s or 2-by-6s spaced ⅛ inch apart for good drainage. The boards are normally nailed to 2-by-6 or 2-by-8 joists spaced 16 inches on center.

If a floorboard is cupped, install it hollow-side down to help prevent water from pooling on the floor.

TOOLS
- Tape measure
- Chalk line
- Hammer
- Wrench
- Handsaw
- Circular saw
- 1x3 guide
- Electric drill

MATERIALS
- 2x4 or 2x6 floorboards
- 2x6 or 2x8 beams and joists
- Plywood cleats (¾")
- Galvanized common nails (2½", 3", 3½")
- Lag screws (⅜"x3½") and washers
- Joist hangers and nails

LAYING A PERMANENT WOOD FlOOR

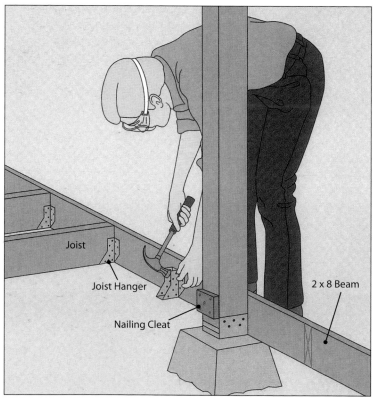

Joist

Joist Hanger

Nailing Cleat

2 x 8 Beam

1. BUILDING THE UNDERSTRUCTURE.

Attach 2-by-8 beams to the outsides of the posts with ⅜-by-3½-inch lag screws.

Mark joist positions every 16 inches along the beams.

With 2½-inch galvanized common nails, attach ¾-inch plywood nailing cleats to the posts level with the beams so the cleats will support the deck boards.

Secure joist hangers to the beams with joist hanger nails *(left)*, then attach the joists to the hangers.

From joist lumber cut bridging boards to fit between joists. Fasten the bridging with 3½-inch nails, offsetting the boards for ease of nailing.

2. FASTENING THE FLOORBOARDS.

Notch floorboards with a handsaw, as necessary, to fit around the posts.

Fasten the first row of boards flush with the beam edge and extending at least 2 inches beyond the understructure, driving two 3-inch nails at each joist position.

Nail down the rest of the floor, spacing boards 5 inch apart. Extend each row at least 2 inches beyond the understructure. Center any end-to-end joints between boards over a joist.

To ensure the edge of the last board is flush with the beam, adjust the spacing between the last 3 feet of boards *(right)*—or trim ¼ inch off the edge of one or more boards—as necessary.

3. TRIMMING THE BOARD ENDS.

Mark the ends of the boards with a chalk line.

Align the blade of your circular saw with the chalk line, butt a 1-by-3 against the base plate, and tack the strip to the deck boards as a cutting guide.

Trim the first 12 inches with a handsaw—the power saw's motor will keep the blade from reaching any closer to the post—then cut along the chalk line with a circular saw *(left)* until the saw contacts the far post. Keep the saw base plate flush against the cutting guide throughout.

Finish the job with a handsaw.

PUTTING TOGETHER A PORTABLE PLATFORM

MAKING DUCKBOARD DECKING.

Measure the length and width of your structure and calculate the quantity and size of duckboards you will need. The usual size is around 3 to 4 foot square.

Build an understructure by butt-nailing pressure-treated 2-by-4s with 3½-inch nails.

Face-nail 2-by-6 boards onto the frame, spacing them ¼ inch apart.

Adjust spacing of the last few boards so that the outermost board fits the end of the frame precisely.

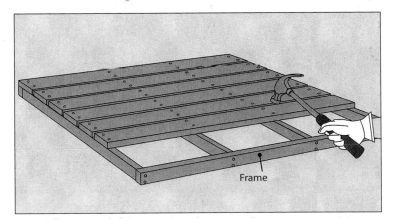

ERECTING SLOPING ROOFS

For small-scale post-and-beam structures, roof rafters can be measured and marked in position. Lumber sizes given in this section are guidelines; consult the building code in your area for possible variations. For an open roof like the ones shown on page 88, buy pressure-treated wood for all the parts.

A SHED ROOF

This type of roof is defined as one that slopes because one side of the structure is built higher than the other. To calculate how much higher, start with the desired roof pitch, which in the example below is 1-in-12 (or 1 inch of rise for every foot of roof width). In this method, the 2-by-6 rafters butt against the crossbeam on the high side, but one-half their width (2⅝ inches) fits into notches cut in the lower crossbeam. You will need to add this amount to the high side, or subtract it from the low side, when building the sides.

A GABLE ROOF

In this type of roof, the rafters rest on beams and meet at a 1-by-8 ridge beam, which forms the peak of the roof. This type of roof is easier to lay out than the shed because the sides are built at the same height. A simple marking guide (*page 96*) will enable you to mark the rafters accurately with no calculation or guesswork.

BRACING WITH COLLAR TIES

Both types of roof suffer an inherent weakness. Since the rafters meet the beams at an angle, their weight and the loads they bear tend to push the sides outward. This can be overcome with collar ties. Brace a shed roof by attaching 2-by-6 collar ties to each pair of end posts, as shown on page 97, with ⅜-by-3½ inch lag screws. For gable roofs, which are more prone to spreading, join every third pair of rafters with a collar tie.

A SHED ROOF

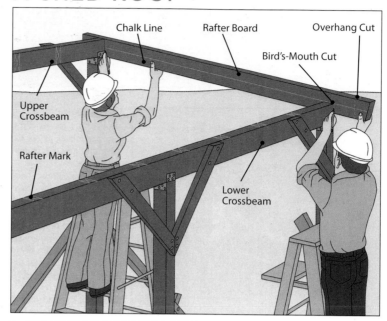

Chalk Line · Rafter Board · Overhang Cut · Bird's-Mouth Cut · Upper Crossbeam · Rafter Mark · Lower Crossbeam

1. MARKING THE RAFTERS.
Make rafter marks 16 inches on center on the crossbeams.

Snap a chalk line down the middle of a rafter board. With a helper, align the board so its top is flush with the top of the upper crossbeam and the chalk line touches the top edge of the lower crossbeam.

Tack the rafter to the upper crossbeam, and outline the edges of the lower crossbeam for a bird's-mouth cut, a notch that fits the rafter snugly to the crossbeam.

Mark along the inner face of the upper crossbeam for the ridge cut, that fits the rafter to the upper crossbeam. With a level, mark a vertical overhang cut on the end of the rafter.

TOOLS
- Tape measure
- Carpenter's level
- Chalk line 1x2, 1x8, 2x6 for marking guide
- Hammer
- Hand saw or saber saw
- Circular saw
- Electric drill

MATERIALS
- 1x2s, 1x4s
- 1 x8 ridge beam
- 2x6 rafters and collar ties
- Galvanized common nails (3", 3½")
- Lag screws (⅜"x3½")
- Multipurpose framing anchors and nails (1½", 2½")

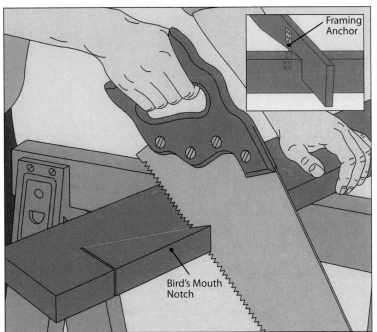

Framing
Anchor

Bird's Mouth
Notch

2. CUTTING AND INSTALLING THE RAFTERS.

Support the rafter on a pair of saw horses and cut along the marked lines with a hand saw *(left)* or a saber saw.

Mark out the remaining rafters, using the cut rafter as a template.

To raise the rafters, toenail them with 3½-inch galvanized common nails to the upper and lower crossbeam at the marked spots.

For additional support, secure each rafter to the lower beam with a multipurpose framing anchor *(inset)* with the nails recommended by the manufacturer.

CUSTOM CUTS FOR RAFTER ENDS

These six patterns are common choices for adding a decorative touch to the plain ends of open-structure rafters. Enlarge the pattern you plan to use on graph paper and transfer it to a rafter. Cut out the patterns with a saber saw, then smooth the shape with medium-grit sandpaper. Another approach is to make a template of the pattern on 5-inch plywood. You can then cut the rafter ends by pattern-routing.

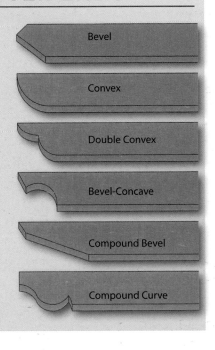

Bevel

Convex

Double Convex

Bevel-Concave

Compound Bevel

Compound Curve

SAFETY TIPS

Wear goggles when nailing and a hard hat when handling materials overhead. Put on gloves when handling pressure-treated wood; add a dust mask when cutting it.

A GABLE ROOF

1. MARKING RAFTERS FOR A GABLE ROOF.

Construct a marking guide by attaching a 1-by-8 upright to the center of a 2-by-6 plank long enough to span the structure. Secure the upright at 90 degrees to the plank with a 1-by-2 brace. Mark the desired height of the peak on the upright.

Set the marking guide on the crossbeams, 1½ inches in from the edge, with the upright centered between the sides. Tack the guide in place.

Check that the upright is plumb and adjust the brace as needed. Snap a chalk line at the center of a rafter board and position the board against the guide as shown *(right)*.

Mark the bird's-mouth cut, the ridge cut, and, with a level, the overhang cut *(page 95)*. Remove the marking guide. Cut the bird's-mouth, ridge, and overhang, then mark and cut the other rafters using the first one as a template.

2. ASSEMBLING THE FRAME.

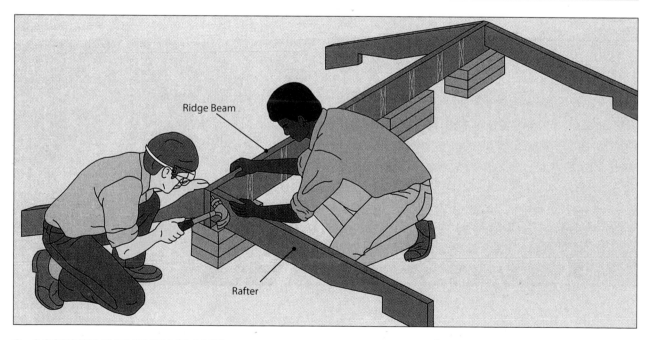

Cut a 1-by-8 ridge beam to the same length as the crossbeams and mark it for rafters every 16 inches.

On one side of the beam, fasten a rafter to each end, nailing through the beam into the end of the rafter with three 3-inch galvanized common nails.

Toenail rafters to the opposite side of the beam *(above)*.

3. POSITIONING THE FRAME.

Brace the end rafters temporarily with 1-by-4s nailed across them.

With three helpers, lift the frame into place, setting the bird's-mouth cuts onto the crossbeams.

If necessary, remove the temporary bracing so you can adjust the fit of the rafters, and replace it when they are correctly positioned.

Toenail the rafters to the crossbeam with 35-inch common nails.

To strengthen the rafter-and-beam joints, add framing anchors with the nails suggested by the manufacturer.

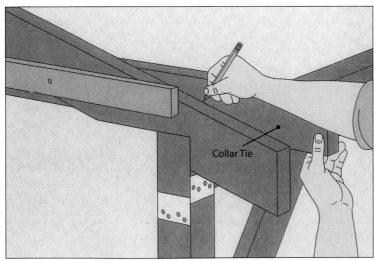

4. FITTING THE COLLAR TIES.

Set a 2-by-6 equal to the width of the structure atop the crossbeams and against a pair of end rafters, and mark it along the top of the rafters.

Cut the board at the marks and use it as a template for the other collar ties.

Nail the collar ties to the end rafters with six 3-inch common nails.

Mount the rest of the rafters, nailing a precut collar beam to every third pair of rafters as you go; then remove the temporary bracing.

A RANGE OF COVERINGS FOR ROOFS AND SIDES

Selecting roofing and siding for an outdoor project depends on the design and intended use of the structure. Storage sheds are best sheathed in weatherproof materials, whereas lawn pavilions and shade houses can be left virtually open— although lattice can be added for privacy or shade. Hybrid designs, such as a waterproof roof with open sides or an open roof with solid sides, expand the range of choices.

Each of these choices is applied over a base of plywood sheathing. A simpler alternative is corrugated plastic paneling.

For an open roof, leave the rafters, with decorative end cuts *(page 95)*, unprotected, or nail crosspieces between them. To provide more shade, you can cover the rafters with latticework or rows of slats, lattice, or shade cloth.

ROOFING MATERIALS

Outdoor structures can be enclosed in much the same manner as houses. Rainproof options range from traditional shingle or clapboard to inexpensive, quick-to-install roll roofing.

SIDING MATERIALS

You can install these same materials, along with bamboo shades, as siding for an outdoor structure. Or, cover open walls with screening to let in light and air—and exclude insects.

A RAFT OF ROOFING MATERIALS

The materials shown below are all appropriate choices for a waterproof roof. Cedar shakes and shingles are rustic and traditional, and typically last 20 to 25 years. Asphalt shingles are probably easier to install, with a lifespan of 15 to 20 years depending on their weight. Corrugated panels (whether of fiberglass or steel) have the advantage of not needing a sheathing under-layment. Translucent panels seal out the elements, but do admit a certain amount of light.

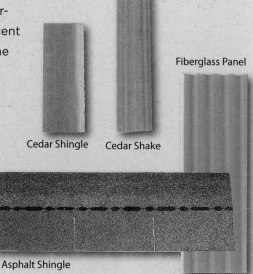

Cedar Shingle   Cedar Shake

Fiberglass Panel

Asphalt Shingle

TOOLS
- Tape measure
- Combination square
- Hammer
- Utility knife
- Handsaw
- Circular saw
- Mason's trowel
- Broom

MATERIALS
- 1x1s, 1x2s, 2x4s, ½" plywood
- Molding (½" x 1)
- Galvanized common nails (2¼" 2½", 3", 3½")
- Galvanized finishing nails (2")
- Galvanized roofing nails (1¼")
- Roll roofing
- Roofing cement

SIMPLE WATERPROOF ROOFING

1. SETTING ROLL ROOFING.

Nail ½-inch plywood sheathing to the rafters, driving 2½-inch common nails at 6-inch intervals.

With 1¼-inch roofing nails, fasten the upper edge of a strip of roll roofing to the sheathing so that the lower edge projects beyond the eave by ½ inch. Fold the roofing up and spread a 12-inch-wide strip of roofing cement on the sheathing along the eave *(right)*.

Press the strip firmly in place and nail its lower edge down.

Work your way up the roof, lapping each new strip over the one in place by 4 inches. On a gable roof, trim the last strips even with the ridge, cutting with a utility knife, then set ridge pieces *(Step 2)*. On a shed roof, lap the last strip over the eave by 5 inches and fasten it to the crossbeam.

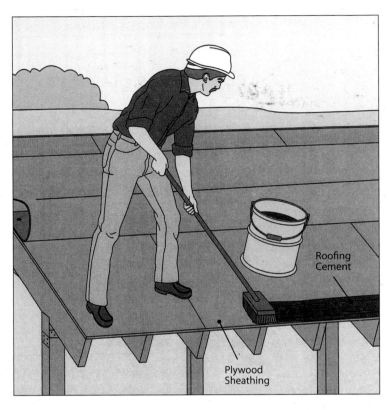

Roofing Cement

Plywood Sheathing

2. COVERING THE RIDGE.

Cut pieces of roll roofing 12 by 36 inches and cement them along the ridge *(left)*. Overlap the ends of the pieces by 6 inches. After pressing down each piece, nail it to the sheathing within 6 inches of the end. Then set the next piece, concealing the nailheads.

AIRY SHEATHING: EASY TO MOUNT

Outdoor structures meant only for warm weather can be graced with a wide range of lightweight and inexpensive roofing and siding materials. Bamboo, woven reed, shade cloth, and corrugated plastic are suitable for structures like trellises and tree houses because they require minimal support and are attached quickly. Shade cloth is particularly suitable for sheltering shade-loving plants. It is available in a variety of weaves that admit different amounts of light. Woven reed and bamboo are normally employed to cover outdoor living spaces.

SHADE CLOTH

The easiest of these materials to install is shade cloth made of synthetic fiber; the polypropylene type is durable and lightweight. Shade cloth must be specially ordered through a nursery or garden shop, which will cut it to size, reinforce the sides, and install grommets to your specifications. Order the cloth so the finished size is 2 inches less all around than your roof *(right)*. Ask for reinforced edges and No. 2 brass grommets.

CORRUGATED PANELS

Corrugated plastic panels are more difficult to install. Furring strips must first be nailed to the rafters and special filler strips attached at the top and bottom—but they do provide rain protection. They should be installed on a roof with a minimum pitch of 1 inch to 1 foot or, in a snowfall area, a pitch of at least 3 inches to 1 foot.

Make sure that any wood you purchase to mount your sheathing is pressure-treated.

TOOLS
- Hammer
- Pliers
- Heavy-duty shears
- Circular saw
- Abrasive blade
- Electric drill
- Heavy-duty stapler
- Handsaw
- Wire cutters

MATERIALS
- 1x1s, 2x2s
- Lumber for fascia, cross supports
- Galvanized common roofing nails (1¾") with rubber washers
- Galvanized wood screws (3" No. 8)
- Screw eyes (2")
- Galvanized wire

A SHADE CLOTH COVER

Screw Eye   Grommet

LACING A SHADE CLOTH

Install 2-inch screw eyes at the corners of the roof, stretch the cloth across its opening, and tie the corner grommets to the screw eyes with good-quality nylon cord.

Position screw eyes around the perimeter of the roof, aligning them with the grommets in the cloth.

Tie one end of a length of cord to a corner screw eye and lace the other end through the grommet at the same corner. Continue feeding the cord through all the screw eyes and grommets on one side of the roof, tightening the cord just enough to remove the slack *(above)*.

Lace the opposite side the same way, working with a helper to tighten the cord on both sides and keep the fabric centered on the roof. Tie the cord to the last corner screw eye.

Lace the remaining sides the same way.

A TRANSLUCENT RAINPROOF ROOF

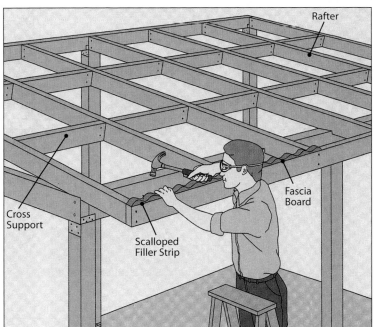

Rafter

Cross
Support

Fascia
Board

Scalloped
Filler Strip

1. ATTACHING FILLER STRIPS.

Install a fascia board the same dimensions as the rafters to the lower ends of the rafters with 3½-inch galvanized common nails. Fasten cross supports between the rafters at 3-foot intervals.

Nail scalloped wooden filler strips across the tops of the fascia board and cross supports with 2-inch nails *(left)*. To ensure that the plastic panels fit properly, keep the filler strips aligned.

Cut half-round filler strips to fit on the rafters between the scalloped filler strips and fasten them in place.

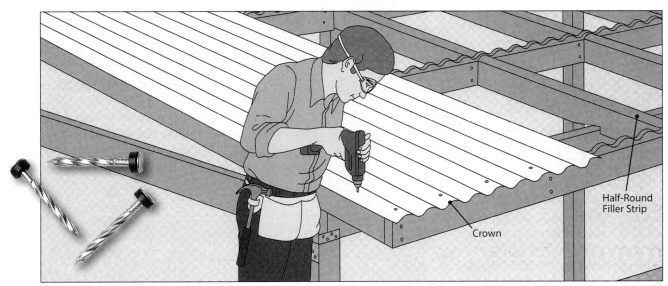

Half-Round
Filler Strip

Crown

2. INSTALLING THE PANELS.

Trim the panels to length with a circular saw equipped with an abrasive blade.

Working on a calm, windless day, position a panel on the roof so one end overlaps the fascia board and one edge overlaps an edge of the roof.

Drill holes ¹⁄₁₆ inch larger than 1¾-inch washered roofing nails through the panels' crowns. Starting at the outside edge *(above)*, drill through every second crown at 12- to 15-inch intervals. Cross supports and upper crossbeam. Do not drill the last crown on the inside edge.

Nail the panel to the filler strips. If you are sheathing a gable roof, add a ridge piece to the peak before driving the top row of nails.

Position the next panel, overlapping the first one by one ridge. Align the bottom ends of the panels, and drill nail holes through both pieces at the same time. Lift the second panel, apply adhesive to the underside of the last ridge of the first panel, and drive the nails.

Install the remaining panels the same way.

COVERING THE ROOF

Many cabins, like most houses, are roofed with asphalt shingles, but two somewhat less common materials may be more appropriate for your cabin or cottage: metal roofing and wooden shakes.

METAL ROOFING

Metal roofing is economical and fire resistant, and for areas subject to heavy snowfalls, it provides a slippery surface that sheds snow before it can build up. Metal panels can be applied to a roof with a pitch of at least 3 inches of vertical rise for every 12 inches of horizontal run. The metal roofing shown here can be purchased in kits, which are available at most farm-equipment and building-supply dealers. The roofing comes in a variety of colors, with panels cut to specified lengths and with specially formed trim pieces or flashings to fit at the eaves, rakes, and ridge. Use a screw gun or drill to drive the appropriate fasteners at the intervals indicated by the manufacturer. The location of sealing strips and the correct overhang of the panels at rakes and eaves will also be indicated.

SHINGLES AND CEDAR SHAKES

Available at home centers or lumberyards, asphalt shingles, wood shingles, and cedar shakes require at least a 4-in-12 slope. Shakes (*pages 104-105*), though expensive, provide the most rustic covering. The methods illustrated on the following pages, simplified from those prescribed for year-round homes, are suitable for vacation and weekend cottages in moderate climates. A starter course of smooth-surfaced shingles is laid along the eaves, and the rest of the roof is covered with rough hand-split shakes.

Shakes are laid on an open deck of 1-by-4s spaced at an interval that is ½ inch less than one-half the length of the shakes.

TOOLS
- Electric drill
- Screwdriver bit
- Tin snips
- Hammer
- Utility knife
- Shingler's hatchet

MATERIALS
- 1 x 4s
- Common nails (2½")
- Roofing nails (1¼")
- Hot-dipped galvanized box nails (1½", 2", 3")
- Roofing felt (15- or 30-pound)
- Metal-roofing kit
- Asphalt shingles
- Cedar shakes and shingles

SNOW-SHEDDING METAL

Roofing Felt

Rake

Rake

Eave Drip Edge

1. INSTALLING THE RAKE PANELS.

Starting at the eaves, attach 30-pound roofing felt with 1¼-inch roofing nails, overlapping sheets by 6 inches.

At the eaves, attach the eave drip edge included in the roofing kit with the fasteners provided (*inset*).

Lay a sealing strip on the eave drip edge, parallel to the eave, then place the first metal panel with its end overhanging the eave so it is square to the eave and rake (*above*).

Attach the panel by driving the fasteners supplied through the sealing strip and into the roof. Then fasten the panel along its length, staggering screws along each side at 1- to 2-foot intervals.

Continue installing panels along the rake in the same way until you reach the ridge.

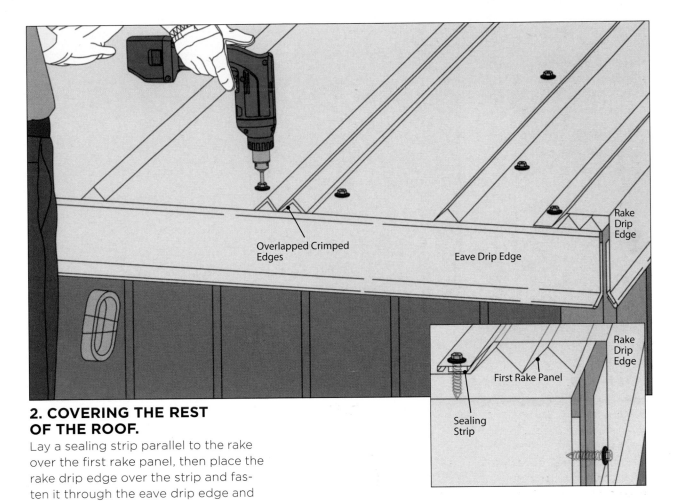

Overlapped Crimped Edges

Eave Drip Edge

Rake Drip Edge

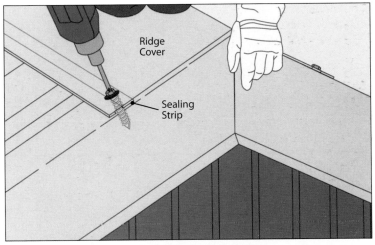

Rake Drip Edge

First Rake Panel

Sealing Strip

2. COVERING THE REST OF THE ROOF.

Lay a sealing strip parallel to the rake over the first rake panel, then place the rake drip edge over the strip and fasten it through the eave drip edge and sealing strip (inset).

To install the other panels, place each one with its crimped edge overlapping the crimped edge on the adjacent panel, and with the overhang of the panels at the eaves equal to that of the first rake panel. Fasten the panels to the roof (above).

If you need more than a single panel length to extend from the eave to the ridge, overlap successive pieces by 3 to 6 feet, installing sealing strips at their ends.

At the opposite rake, cut the last panels with tin snips, if necessary. Install them, then add the sealing strip and rake drip edge along the rake.

Cover the other side of the roof in the same way.

Ridge Cover

Sealing Strip

3. ATTACHING THE RIDGE COVER.

On each side of the ridge, lay a sealing strip parallel to the ridge, then position a ridge cover over the ridge and attach it to the roof by driving the screws through the sealing strips (above).

AN ASPHALT-SHINGLE ROOF

LAYING COURSES OF SHINGLES

Install roofing felt as for a metal roof (*page 102, Step 1*), but lay 15-pound felt.

For the starter course, cut the three tabs off the shingles with a utility knife and remove 6 inches from the first shingle.

With four 1¼-inch roofing nails per shingle, fasten the starter course so the shingles overhang the eaves and rakes by ¼ inch. In each shingle, drive four nails below the line of adhesive (*inset*): one nail above each cutout and one nail 1 inch from each end.

Fasten two shingles of the first course over the starter course.

For the second course, cut half a tab from the first shingle on the end that will abut the rake, nail it down, then attach the second shingle. Install two shingles in the third, fourth, and fifth courses in the same way, starting each one with a shingle cut half a tab shorter than the course below to create a stepped pattern on the roof.

Lay the sixth course by nailing a half-tab to the roof, then adding a full

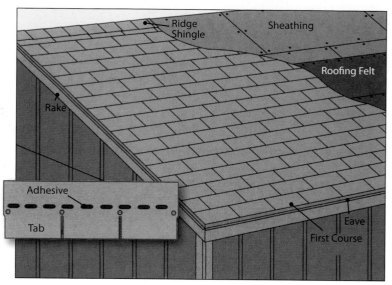

shingle. At the seventh course, repeat the pattern used for the first six courses. When you reach the rake, return to the eaves and add two-full size shingles to each course. Continue the process to cover the roof; trim the last course of shingles even with the ridge.

Finish the ridge with individual shingle tabs bent to cover both sides, starting with a tab at each end of the roof ¼ inch beyond the rakes; working toward the middle, overlap succeeding tabs by 7 inches. Trim the top end of the last tab so at least 5 inches of the tab it covers is exposed. Bend a half tab in two and nail it over the two tabs that overlap at the middle of the ridge.

LAYING DOWN SHAKES

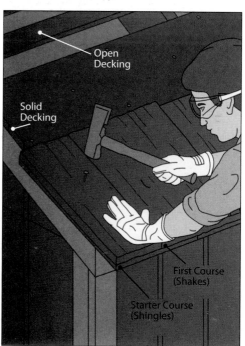

1. LAYING A DOUBLE STARTER COURSE.

For the first 3 feet up from the eave, install solid decking—1-by-4s fastened edge to edge to the rafters with 2½-inch common nails. Continue up to the ridge laying open decking. At the ridge butt the last two rows of decking boards together.

Cover the solid decking with 30-pound roofing felt, securing it with 1¼-inch roofing nails.

With 1½-inch hot-dipped galvanized box nails, fasten a starter course of cedar shingles, overhanging the eave by 2 inches and the rakes by 1½ inches.

Nail an 18-inch-wide strip of roofing felt over the shingles, 10 inches above the eave.

Driving 2-inch box nails with a shingler's hatchet, lay the first course of shakes over the shingles, aligning the ends, but offsetting vertical joints by at least 1½ inches (*left*).

2. LAYING THE REMAINING COURSES.

Cut a scrap shake to the length of the gap between decking boards—8½ inches for 18-inch shakes; 11½ inches for 24-inch shakes—and use it to align the bottom of each shake with that of the shake in the course below.

Lay an 18-inch strip of roofing felt with its lower edge halfway between the top of the starter course and the bottom of the next course.

Fasten the second course of shakes with two 2-inch box nails (right).

Lay another strip of felt, then another course of shakes. Continue in this way to the ridge.

With 3-inch box nails, cover the ridge with special two-piece ridge shakes: Start by doubling the ridge shakes at one end, then overlap the shakes as you move along the ridge to the other end so the corner joints alternate from one side of the ridge to the other (inset).

Corner Joint

MAKING SHAKES.

You may want to cut your own shakes from cedar or redwood logs. To do so, saw a log into 16-inch sections and mark lines at ¼-inch intervals across the end of the section. Place the log on wood blocks, hold a froe—a special cutter available from specialty-tool suppliers—with its sharp edge against the top of the log, and strike the blade sharply with a wooden mallet (right), splitting the shake from the log. Do not try to cut through a knot; instead, remove the froe and move to the next mark on the log.

THE A-FRAME: A TENT BUILT WITH PLYWOOD

One of the simplest of all buildings takes the form of a braced triangle—an A-frame—rising from the ground. The rafters serve as both roof and walls and enclose a structure that is practical for many types of small outdoor buildings. A low A-frame, with a peak 3 to 5 feet above the ground, might be used as a pet shelter or a storage shed; a higher one, with 6 or more feet of headroom, can serve as a garden house, playroom, or studio.

RAFTER LENGTH

In every A-frame, the walls that form the roof are of equal length, but the angle at the peak may vary considerably, affecting both headroom and floor space. A typical A-frame, like the one on these pages, is an equilateral triangle, with a base and sides of the same length. A-frames with steeper sides have more headroom, but proportionately less floor space; flattening the triangle has the opposite effect.

PLANNING THE FOUNDATION

As long as the A-frame is kept relatively small—less than 12 feet high—it does not need a full foundation extending below the frost line. It can rest on a concrete slab (below) or on concrete piers (page 86). Smaller buildings can rest directly on level ground or on a bed of gravel. Like the rafters of a roof truss, the A-frame rafters will tend to spread unless they are tied together. One way to secure them is by fastening floor joists to the rafters. This works well for a playhouse or a garden shed. Another method is to bolt the sole plates to the slab.

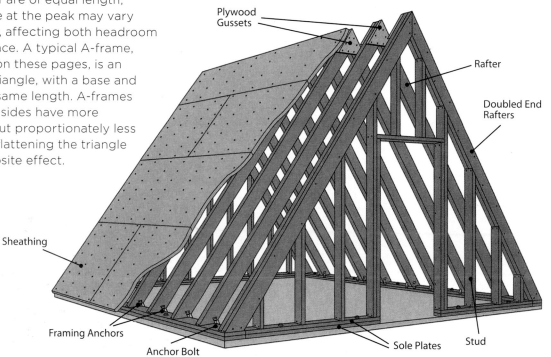

Plywood Gussets

Rafter

Doubled End Rafters

Sheathing

Framing Anchors

Anchor Bolt

Sole Plates

Stud

ANATOMY OF AN A-FRAME

The rafters of this typical A-frame are 2-by-6s joined at their peaks with triangular plywood gussets. (The gussets on the outermost side of the doubled end rafters are omitted so the sheathing will lie flat against the vertical walls.) Multipurpose framing anchors connect the base of each rafter to the 2-by-8 sole plates bolted to the concrete slab. The end walls are framed with conventional 2-by-4 sole plates and studding, and the entire structure is covered with plywood sheathing and a weatherproof covering.

A VERSATILE STRUCTURE

Large outbuildings like the one shown below can serve as garages, storage areas, studios, workshops, or some combination of all of these. Almost any purpose can be accommodated, even living quarters. Each use, however, has requirements that should be considered early in the planning process.

A garage needs a driveway, walkways, a main entrance, and perhaps a side door. The floor must be sloped for drainage. For garden storage, include a door that provides easy access to the garden. A studio or shop should have windows, and possibly a loft for storage. If you need electricity and water, consult your local utility companies about preparing the structure for their installation.

PLANNING THE CONSTRUCTION

Draw a floor plan of the building on a map of your property to ensure it is located at least as far from the house and the property lines as local codes require. Then sketch front and side views of the building on graph paper to determine whether the building will harmonize with the main house and surrounding property. You will probably need a building permit.

Bring along your diagrams and sketches, and be prepared to describe the type of foundation, wall construction, and roof design that you propose. Some localities require a soil test to determine whether it will support the proposed structure. And set up an inspection schedule well in advance so that work will not be delayed.

> **CAUTION**
> *Before excavating, establish the locations of underground obstacles such as electric, water, and sewer lines, and dry wells, septic tanks, and cesspools.*

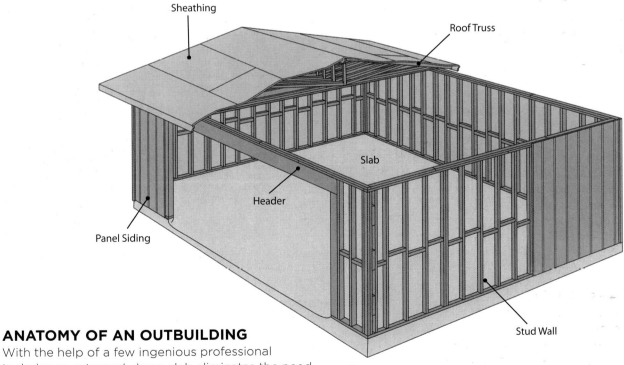

Sheathing

Roof Truss

Panel Siding

Header

Slab

Stud Wall

ANATOMY OF AN OUTBUILDING

With the help of a few ingenious professional techniques, a turned-down slab eliminates the need for costly forms or uncommon masonry skills; stud walls *(pages 108-112)* can be built on the ground and erected as units; and prefabricated trusses (page 114), which require no tricky rafter cuts or a ridge beam, make the installation of a sloping roof a simple assembly process.

STURDY WALLS: ASSEMBLED FLAT THEN TILTED UP

Stud walls provide a sturdy framework suitable for any structure, from a shed to a garage. The method is simple: Evenly spaced studs are nailed to top plates, then the walls are tilted upright in sections and the studs are toenailed to sole plates.

HEADER BEAMS

At each door or window opening, the roof load is carried by a horizontal header supported at its ends by posts or studs. For most headers, a board-and-plywood sandwich 3½ inches thick and up to 11½ inches wide is generally appropriate. Check your code requirements. Wider spans like the garage door opening shown below may require an engineered wood such as laminated veneer lumber (LVL). A wood dealer can tell you the required size; two pieces of LVL can be fastened together to create a thicker beam.

FOLLOWING A PLAN

Draw a set of plans to show the building inspector when you apply for a permit and for reference as you work. Start by drawing a simple floor plan on graph paper; indicate the overall dimensions of the structure, the distance between the center of each opening and the nearest corner of the building, and the size of each rough opening (usually specified by the manufacturer of the finished door or window). Then draw head-on views of the walls that have openings; indicate the height of the walls, the height and span of each opening and the sizes of the studs, posts, and headers that will support the roof.

Use the plan to determine exactly what materials you need when you order lumber. Studs—generally 2-by-4s cut 8 feet long at the sawmill—are usually spaced 16 inches apart. The 2-by-4 top plates should be straight pieces of structural-grade lumber at least 14 feet long.

BRACING THE WALLS

Plumb the walls accurately and brace them firmly. The temporary braces must hold the entire structure rigid while the roof trusses are put in. When the roof has been sheathed, remove the braces one by one as you apply the wall sheathing.

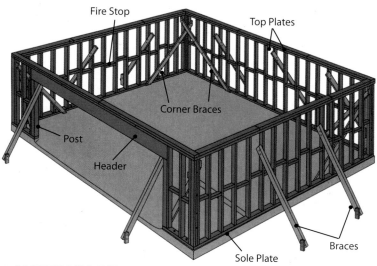

ANATOMY OF STUD-WALL FRAMING

In the structure shown above, the studs are nailed to the bottom layer of the top plates then to the sole plates. The second layer of the top plates ties the walls together at the corners and at the joints in the first layer. Temporary diagonal bracing holds the walls and corners plumb. The long span of the garage door is bridged with an LVL header supported by 4-by-4 posts. Horizontal 2-by-4 fire stops nailed between the studs are required in some areas; they add rigidity to the structure and provide a nailing surface for exterior sheathing.

TOOLS
- Tape measure
- Carpenter's square
- Carpenter's level
- Plumb bob
- Hammer
- Chisel
- Mallet
- Circular saw

MATERIALS
- 2x4s
- 4x4s
- LVL Beams
- Common nails (3", 3½")

PREPARING THE SOLE AND TOP PLATES

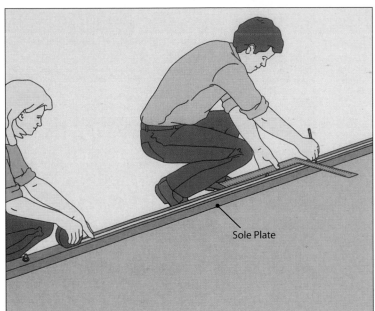

1. MARKING THE STUDS ON THE SOLE PLATES.

Drive a nail into the sole plate of a side wall 15¼ inches from the outside of the back wall.

Holding the tongue of a carpenter's square across the sole plate at the nail, run a pencil along both edges of the tongue, outlining the first stud location.

Hook a long tape measure on the nail and outline the next stud 16 inches from the first, while a helper holds the tape taut *(left)*.

Mark the remaining stud locations at 16-inch intervals on all the sole plates. On each side of the garage door opening, mark the 4-by-4 posts.

Sole Plate

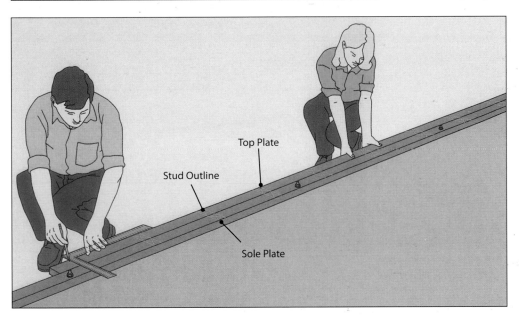

Top Plate

Stud Outline

Sole Plate

2. MARKING THE TOP PLATES.

Working with a helper, butt a top plate against the sole plate with the ends flush at a corner.

Transfer the stud outlines from the sole plates to the top plates with a carpenter's square *(above)*.

With a circular saw, trim the ends of top plates in the middle of stud outlines to ensure that seams in the plate are centered over a stud.

Make sure that sections of the top plate abutting a corner are at least 8 feet long and perfectly aligned with the end of the sole plate.

RAISING THE WALLS

1. NAILING STUDS TO THE TOP PLATE.

Build and raise the back and side walls (*Steps 1-3*) then the front one (*Step 4*).

Lay studs on edge on the slab—one for each outline on the sole plate—and position a top plate along the tops.

Stand on the stud and top plate, align the stud with its outline, and drive two 3½-inch common nails through the plate into the stud. If a stud aligns with a seam in the top plate, center the joint on the stud, and angle the nails toward its middle.

For a stud that lines up with an anchor bolt in the sole plate, notch the stud with a chisel to fit over the bolt.

2. PREPARING CORNER POSTS.

For each corner, sandwich three, evenly spaced 18-inch-long 2-by-4s between two studs and fasten the assembly together with 3½-inch nails *(right)*, making a corner post.

Nail the post to the end of one of the top plates at each corner *(inset)*.

3. ERECTING THE WALLS.

With one helper for every 8 feet of wall, tilt one wall upright.

Set the studs on their marks on the sole plate and brace the wall with long 2-by-4s at 6-foot intervals, keeping the wall roughly vertical with a carpenter's level.

Toenail each stud to the bottom plate with 3-inch nails, driving two fasteners from one side of the stud and one from the other.

At each corner, face-nail the outside stud of one wall to the corner post of the adjoining wall, tying them together.

Stud
Top Plate

Corner Post

Corner Post

4. FASHIONING THE FRONT WALL.

Assemble the front-wall sections on either side of the door, nailing studs to top-plate sections that extend over the door opening by at least 3 feet.

Cut two 4-by-4 posts to the height of the wall studs, less the height of the header for the door opening *(page 113)*.

Fasten a stud along the inside edge of each post with 3½-inch nails spaced 10 inches apart in a zigzag pattern *(right)*.

Erect and brace the front wall sections as you did the other walls.

Post

Corner Brace

ALIGNING THE FRAMEWORK

1. PLUMBING THE CORNERS.

Hang a plumb bob from the top plate near a corner so the tip of the bob is slightly above the bottom plate.

Make a corner brace by mitering the ends of a long 2-by-4 at 45-degree angles. With a 3-inch common nail, secure the brace to the last stud of the wall being plumbed so one mitered end is flush with the outside edge of the stud.

With one helper supporting the wall and another eyeing the plumb bob, remove the exterior bracing you set up when raising the wall *(page 110, Step 3)*. Have your helper tilt the wall so that the plumb bob aligns with the edge of the sole plate, then face-nail the brace to the sole plate of the adjoining wall, holding its bottom end against the slab *(left)*.

Plumb the other walls the same way.

2. STRAIGHTENING THE WALLS.

Nail a 2-by-4 block to the inside edge of the top plate at each end of one wall.

Drive a nail into one end of each block and stretch a string tautly between the nails and across the face of each block.

Working on a stepladder near the middle of the wall, hold a scrap 2-by-4 between the string and the top plate. If there is a gap between the string and the board, or if the board pushes out the string, have one helper tilt the wall as necessary while another reinstalls exterior bracing to hold the wall in position (right).

Straighten the other walls this way.

Exterior Brace · 2 x 4 Spacer · 2 x 4 Block

3. COMPLETING THE TOP PLATE.

To reinforce the corners, arrange the second top-plate layer so the boards overlap as shown at left.

Position a 2-by-4 over the first top-plate layer, aligning one end with the outside edge of the adjoining wall. Cut the other end so it is at least 4 feet from a joint in the first layer.

Nail the second top-plate board to the lower one with 3½-inch common nails spaced every 8 inches in a zigzag pattern. At the corners, drive two nails where the top layer overlaps the bottom one of the adjoining wall (left).

Continue nailing the second top-plate layer around the perimeter, except over the door opening where the header must be installed first (opposite).

Nail the corner braces to every stud they cross with 3-inch nails.

Corner Braces

BRIDGING THE DOOR OPENING

1. BUILDING THE HEADER.

For a span over 8 feet, cut a length of LVL lumber to fit between the studs at the edges of the door opening.

For a double header, you can nail two lengths of LVL together face to face, staggering 3½-inch common nails along both sides at 10-inch intervals (*right*). Or, order an LSL (laminated structural lumber) beam as required for your span.

For a span up to 8 feet, build a header from a pair of 2-by-12s with a strip of ½-inch plywood of the same width and length sandwiched between them. Nail the header as you would a doubled LVL beam, adding construction adhesive to the surfaces that will be in contact.

LVL Lumber

Header

2. LIFTING THE HEADER INTO PLACE.

With one helper for every 5 feet of header length, lift the header and slide it onto the posts at the edges of the door opening. The typical header is a manageable load for four people.

Have your helpers hold the ends of the header in place while you fasten it to the studs adjoining the posts, the posts themselves, and the top-plate sections with 3½-inch nails.

Finish installing the lower top-plate layer, then nail the upper top-plate layer over the door opening.

READY-MADE TRUSSES TO SUPPORT THE ROOF

The most rapid and economical way to frame the roof of a rectangular structure is to install prefabricated trusses. In addition to eliminating the need for heavy structural joists and rafters, trusses save you from having to cut rafters at complex angles and erecting a ridge beam.

TRUSS PARTS

Trusses typically consist of three chords—the pieces that form the triangular shape— and webs that fit between the chords to support the top chords and transfer stress to the bottom chord and to the exterior bearing walls. The corners of a truss are joined with metal gussets.

PURCHASING TRUSSES

When ordering trusses, specify the span between the exterior walls, the length of the overhang, and the type of end cut—plumb or square—you desire. Also specify the pitch of the roof. The standard pitch for trusses spaced at 24-inch intervals is 4 inches to 1 foot, but local codes in areas with heavy snowfall may require a greater pitch or more closely spaced trusses. Consult your local building code for this information.

Installing the Framing: Trusses rely on sheathing for stability. In areas with little snow, ¼-inch plywood is acceptable. In others, ½- to ⅝ -inch may be required. Check the code. In either case, bolster the joints with plywood sheathing clips *(page 120)*.

You will need at least three helpers to lift, roll, and secure the trusses. When lifting the trusses, carry them in a vertical position with one helper at each end. Trusses can be damaged easily if mishandled.

The final step involves weather-proofing and adding ventilation.

TOOLS
- Tape measure
- Carpenter's square
- Chalk line
- Carpenter's level
- Hammer
- Maul
- Handsaw
- Circular saw
- Saber saw

MATERIALS
- 1x6s, 2x4s
- Plywood sheathing
- Plywood panel siding
- Prefabricated roof trusses
- Common nails (2½", 3", 3½")
- Galvanized common nails (2½, 3¼", 3½")
- Plywood sheathing clips
- String

A RANGE OF TRUSS STYLES

Truss construction is largely dictated by local conditions. Queen is a common style, but Howe might be found in an area with high snowfall. If you plan to build a catwalk above the bottom chords for storage, order trusses without a center web, such as the Fink. You will need two gable end trusses with webs spaced 16 inches apart for attaching the sheathing. Because these trusses rest on a wall, their webs can be modified to create framing for a ventilation opening. A truss manufacturer or distributor will suggest the right trusses for your project.

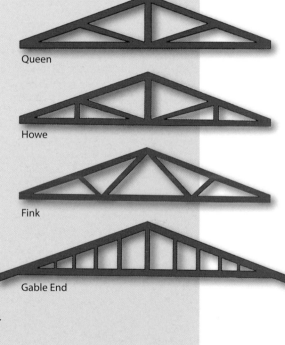

Queen

Howe

Fink

Gable End

PREPARING THE WALLS FOR TRUSSES

1. MARKING THE TRUSS LOCATIONS.

If required by your building code, add 2-by-4 fire stops, staggering their heights so you can face-nail them to the studs with 3½-inch common nails.

Standing on a scaffold, measure 24¾ inches from a side wall and mark a line across the front wall's top plate with a carpenter's square. Mark a second line 1½ inches away to outline the truss location.

Outline the remaining truss positions on 24-inch centers, using the first mark as a starting point *(left)*.

Repeat the process to lay out truss locations on the back wall.

Truss Location

Over-hang

2. LAYING OUT THE OVERHANG.

To assist in positioning the trusses, set up a layout line along the front wall. To do so:

Nail a 2-by-4 to the outside face of each side wall top plate with 35-inch common nails so the tops of the board and the top plate are flush. Attach the board so it projects beyond the truss overhang by a few inches.

Mark the overhang on each 2-by-4, then tie a string tautly between the marks *(above)*.

Nailer

2 x 4 Spacer

3. FASTENING THE NAILERS.

Secure boards to the side-wall top plates as nailing surfaces for the bottom chords of the end trusses.

Attach 2-by-4 nailers to the top plates with 3-inch nails; hold a 2-by-4 spacer on edge on the top plate while fastening to offset the front edges of the nailer and top plate by 1½ inches *(left)*.

Trim the nailers flush with the front and back walls.

4. ERECTING THE SCABS.

Prepare four 8-foot-long 2-by-4 braces—or "scabs"—to align and hold the end trusses even with the edge of the top plates. Since siding is applied to end trusses before they are raised, attach a 4-foot strip ot siding to each scab as a spacer *(inset)*.

Attach two scabs to each side wall with 3-inch common nails *(left)*. Position the scabs about one-third of the way in from the front and back walls; set their height so the top end of the siding spacer is flush with the top plate of the wall.

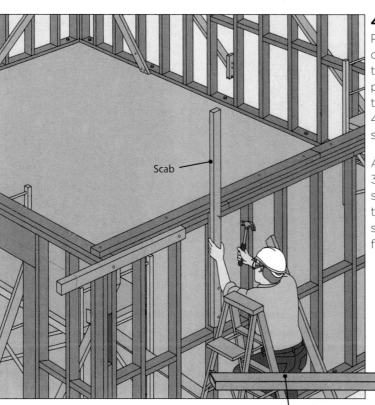

Scab

2 x 4 Scab

Siding Spacer

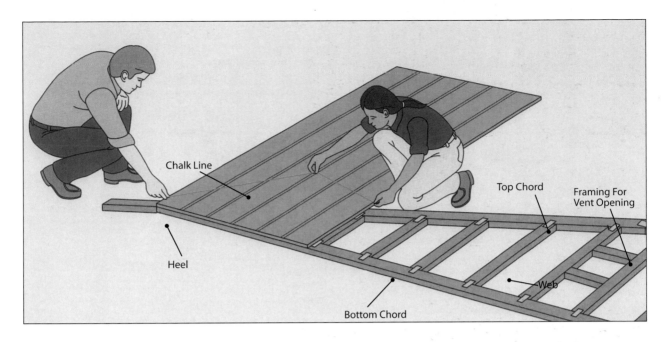

5. SHEATHING THE END TRUSSES.

Install framing in the end trusses for a roof vent.

Set an end truss on the ground and lay a 4-by-8 sheet of plywood siding on it, aligning a corner of the sheet with the heel—or bottom corner—at one end of the truss.

Snap a chalk line across the siding in line with the top chord of the truss *(above)*, then cut the siding along the line.

Nail the cut section of siding to the truss with galvanized box nails long enough to penetrate 1 inch into the truss.

Fasten siding to the rest of the truss the same way, then cut the vent opening with a saber saw.

RAISING THE ROOF

1. HOISTING AN END TRUSS.

With two helpers, carry an end truss upside down into the building. Then, standing on a scaffold, lift one end until the top chord rests on the top plate of one side wall *(left)*.

With your helpers on another scaffold, pivot the other end of the truss onto the opposite side wall top plate.

2. INSTALLING THE END TRUSS.

Have a helper wedge a 2-by-4 into the peak of the truss and tilt it upright *(above)*. With another helper on the scaffold, guide the truss so the bottom chord settles between the nailer and the scabs.

Align the front-wall end of the truss with the overhang line along the front wall.

On a ladder outside the building, nail the scabs to the top chord of the truss and drive a 3½-inch galvanized common nail through the siding and the bottom chord of the truss into the nailer every 16 inches.

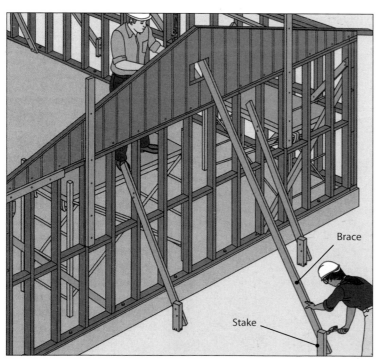

3. PLUMBING THE END TRUSS.

Support the end truss with a 16-foot-long 2-by-4 brace, nailing one end of the brace to the vent opening framing and the other to a 2-by-4 stake driven into the ground about 8 feet from the wall.

Loosen the scabs and position a carpenter's level against the top and bottom chords of the end truss. Meanwhile, have a helper reposition the brace on the stake so that the end truss is plumb *(left)*.

A TRUSS POLE

Tilting an unsheathed truss into position with a 2-by-4 stud can be dangerous—as the truss pivots, the board can slip off, allowing the truss to strike you in the face. The solution is to make a simple Y-shaped truss pole like this one by fastening a 1-by-4 to the stud with 2-inch wood screws.

4. INSTALLING TRUSS BRACING.

Tilt the second truss into position over its outlines on the top plates and align an end with the overhang line.

Toenail the truss to the top plates with 3¼-inch galvanized common nails. Attach a multipurpose framing anchor *(photograph)* to each end of the truss with the nails recommended by the manufacturer.

Outline the truss spacing on an 8-foot-long 1-by-6 brace for each side of the ridge and fasten one end of the brace to the end truss with two 2½-inch nails. Aligning the truss with the first outline, nail the brace to the top chord *(right)*. Repeat on the other side of the ridge.

5. RAISING THE REMAINING TRUSSES.

Position and brace the rest of the trusses except the last four. Install more braces as needed, fastening them to trusses already in place *(above)*.

Install the remaining end truss.

Tilt the last three trusses up to the roof before positioning any of them. Then position and brace them one at a time.

6. SHEATHING THE TRUSSES.

Set up the scaffolds along the side walls. With a helper, snap chalk lines along the top chords of the trusses 4 and 8 feet from the overhang as guidelines for laying plywood sheathing.

Align the top edge of a 4-by-8 sheet of sheathing with the chalk line and center it over the fifth truss.

As a helper slips a plywood clip onto the top edge of the sheathing between each truss, secure the sheet with 2½-inch galvanized common nails every 6 inches along the top chords (right).

After sheathing the bottom 4 feet of the roof, remove the braces fastened to the trusses and cover the next 4 feet, starting the row with a half-sheet in order to stagger the joints from the bottom row.

Before installing the last row of sheets, trim their top edges so the sheathing stops 1 inch short of the ridge. Cover the other side of the trusses the same way.

Plywood Clip

7. STABILIZING THE BOTTOM CHORDS.

On each side of the ridge, support the bottom chords of the trusses with the bracing you removed in Step 6. Position a brace across the trusses and, holding the chord in line with its outline, attach the brace to the truss with two 2½-inch nails (left).

If your area experiences high wind, diagonal bracing may be required; check the local building code.

Truss Outline

SIDING WITH PLYWOOD

Plywood siding is sturdy, economical, and easy to install. Designed to face the elements, it comes in various lengths—but 8 feet is most common—and in a variety of textures and patterns. It is also available with shiplap edges that mesh with adjoining panels.

If your studs are 24 inches apart, make sure the paneling is the thicker kind designed for this spacing. When ordering the paneling, ask your supplier for Z-flashing to fit between the end-truss siding and the wall siding.

TOOLS
- Caulking gun
- Hammer
- Tin snips
- Circular saw

MATERIALS
- 1x3s, 1x4s
- Plywood siding panels
- Z-flashing
- Exterior caulk
- Galvanized box nails
- Galvanized finishing nails (2¼)

SAFETY TIPS
Wear goggles when nailing.

Z-Flashing

End-Truss Siding

Siding

1. FASTENING THE FIRST PANEL.
Starting at a corner, apply exterior caulk to the stud surfaces that will contact the first panel.

Slip one flange of a piece of Z-flashing behind the sheathing that covers the end truss, then ease the first siding panel behind the other flange *(inset)*.

Secure the panel to the studs with galvanized box nails long enough to penetrate the studs by 1 inch. Space the fasteners 6 inches apart along the starting stud and at 12-inch intervals along the other studs. Rather than driving nails through the lapped edge of the panel, apply caulk along the lap *(left)*.

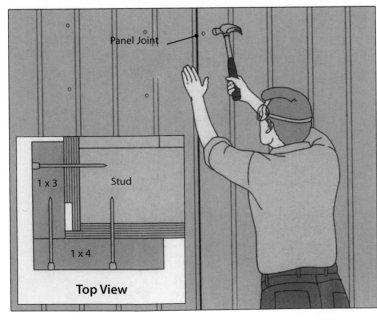

Panel Joint

1 x 3   Stud

1 x 4

Top View

2. FINISHING THE JOB.
Install the next panel so its lapped edge meshes with the first. Avoiding the joint, nail the edge of the second panel to the stud *(left)*; this will leave the first panel free to expand.

Install the rest of the siding this way. Trim the corner panels and Z-flashing as needed using tin snips to cut the flashing.

Cover the exposed edges of the siding at the corners with 1-by-3s and 1-by-4s fastened with 2¼-inch galvanized finishing nails *(inset)*.

A COTTAGE OF PREFAB PANELS

This cottage has standard stud walls covered with siding *(below)*. An advantage to this structure is that its walls can be prefabricated in sections, hauled to the site in a small truck and, with three or four helpers, quickly assembled on the floor of the cabin and topped with a simple rafter or truss roof *(pages 114-120)*.

PLANNING

To ensure that the sections fit together properly, draw a scaled plan of the structure before building the panels. Indicate the size of the foundation and the location and dimensions of walls, doors, and windows. You can simplify construction by ordering doors and windows that fit between studs *(opposite)*. If you are planning to build your cabin with a shed roof, you'll need to make the back wall higher than the front, or one side wall higher than the other.

WALL PANELS

The wall frames are built in multiples of 4 feet—a size that suits common building materials. The economical cabin shown on these pages uses 8-foot exterior siding, and has ceilings just under 7 feet high. If you want higher ceilings, cut the wall studs longer and buy 10-foot siding—which costs a bit more—and trim it to length.

Place the assembled panels on the truck in order so that the last one you load is the first to be erected; this way, you can unload and assemble the walls in sequence.

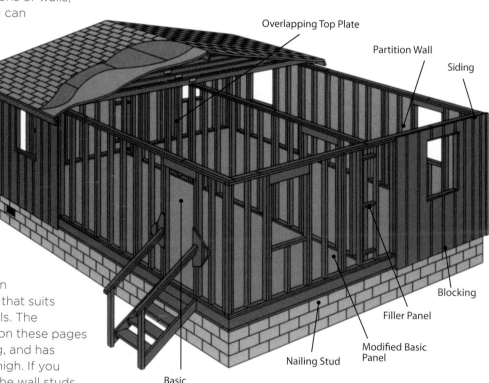

Overlapping Top Plate

Partition Wall

Siding

Blocking

Filler Panel

Modified Basic Panel

Nailing Stud

Basic Panel

ANATOMY OF A PREFAB CABIN

This cabin has wall panels in three sizes. The basic panels are 8 feet wide, the filler and corner panels are 4 feet wide. Modified basic panels at each corner provide a nailing surface for the end stud of the adjoining corner panel. The wall sections are nailed together where they abut, and connected by an overlapping top plate, installed on site. Interior partition walls are framed the same way as the exterior walls, which have blocking where the partitions adjoin them.

THE BASIC PANEL

Each panel is made from seven 2-by-4 studs cut 6 feet 9 inches long. The 2-by-4 top and soleplates are cut 8 feet long, and the studs are fastened to the plates at 16-inch intervals with the middle stud in the center of the panel so wallboard and interior paneling can be nailed there. Two pieces of ⅝-inch vertical siding are nailed to the studs and plates flush with the outside faces of the outer studs so they project above the top plate by 1½ inches and below the soleplate by 10½ inches.

Filler panels are made in the same way, but with four studs and one piece of siding, so they are only 4 feet wide. A basic panel can be adapted to accommodate a window or door as shown for the modified and corner panels below.

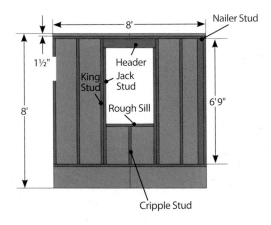

A CORNER PANEL

The top and sole-plates of this panel are 7 feet 8½ inches long, with the stud at the corner spaced only 12½ inches from the next stud. The sheathing overlaps the corner end by 3½ inches. When the panel is put in place, the overlapped siding attaches to the end stud of a modified basic panel. Because the siding always overlaps to the right when viewed from outside, erect the walls from left to right. A door opening is framed much like that of a window, but the rough sill and cripple stud are omitted.

A MODIFIED BASIC PANEL

To tie walls together at a corner, an extra "nailer" stud is added—flush with the inside edge of the sole-plate—at the left end of a basic panel—when viewed from the outside—to serve as a nailing surface for the first stud of the adjoining corner panel. For a panel with a window opening, a header, made with ½-inch plywood nailed between two 2-by-6s, spans the top of the opening; jack studs nailed to the king studs at either side of the opening support the header; a rough sill is toenailed to the jack studs; and a cripple stud braces the rough sill.

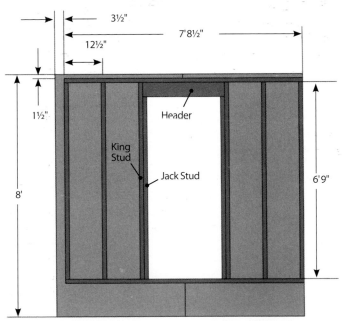

BUILDING WALLS IN SECTIONS

1. SIZING THE STUDS WITH A JIG.

To make a jig that will enable you to cut several studs to length in a single operation, secure a plywood panel atop a pair of sawhorses with 2-inch common nails. With 3-inch nails, attach a 2-by-4 stop along one side of the panel, and a 2-by-2 stop along an end, perpendicular to the side stop. With a hinge, fasten a 2-by-2 guide at a 90-degree angle across the side stop and panel; locate the guide so that the studs will be the correct length when you run a circular saw along it.

Swing the saw guide up and put the 2-by-4s edge to edge in the jig so they are butted against the end stop and the first board is flush against the side stop. Lower the guide in place.

Holding the 2-by-4s steady, run a circular saw across the boards with the base plate against the guide *(above)*.

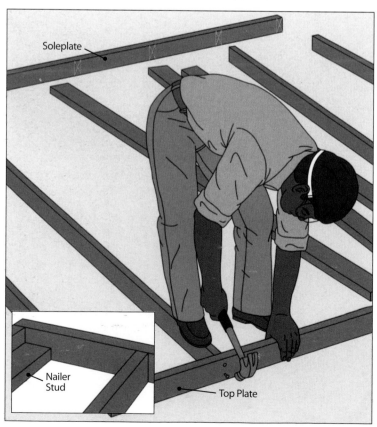

2. JOINING THE STUDS AND PLATES.

Cut the top and soleplates to length, then mark stud locations on one face of each board, placing the middle-stud mark in the center of each plate and the rest at 16-inch intervals. If the panel will have a window or door opening, space the studs on each side of the gap according to the rough opening required, plus 3 inches.

To join the studs and top plate, align the stud with its outline, stand on the board, and drive two 3½-inch common nails through the plate into the stud *(left)*.

Attach the soleplate the same way.

For a modified panel *(page 123, middle)*, add a nailer stud butted against the last stud and flush with the inside of the top and soleplates *(inset)*.

For a corner panel *(page 123, bottom)*, locate the last stud at the corner 12½ inches from the next one.

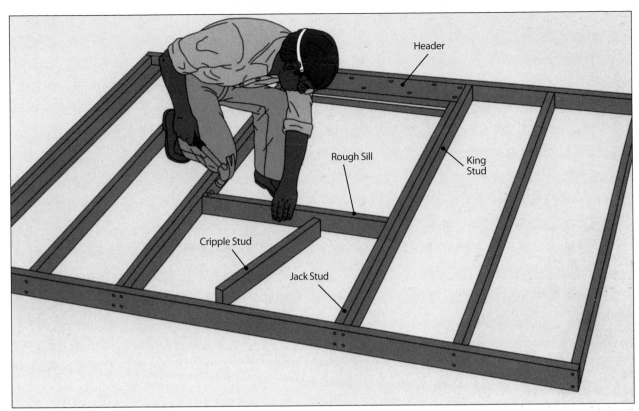

3. FRAMING A ROUGH OPENING FOR A WINDOW.

To make the header, first cut two 2-by-6s and a ½-inch plywood spacer of the same width to fit in the opening; sandwich the spacer between the 2-by-6s and secure the assembly with 3½-inch common nails driven every 10 inches in a staggered pattern.

Cut two jack studs to fit between the header and soleplate, and fasten them to the king studs at each side of the opening.

Cut a 2-by-4 rough sill to fit between the jack studs and fasten it (above), spacing it from the header the distance indicated by the window manufacturer's specifications.

Cut a 2-by-4 cripple stud to fit between the sill and soleplate, then nail it to both boards.

Frame a door opening in the same way, but omit the sill and cripple stud.

4. A JIG FOR FASTENING THE SIDING.

Cut a 2-by-2 stop 8 feet long and nail it along one edge of a plywood panel.

Cut a 2-by-4 stop 3 feet 10½ inches long and fasten it along an end of the panel.

Cut two 1-by-6s to the lengths of the two stops; then, with 2-inch No. 6 wood screws, fasten one to the inside edge of the 2-by-4 and the other to the outside of the 2-by-2.

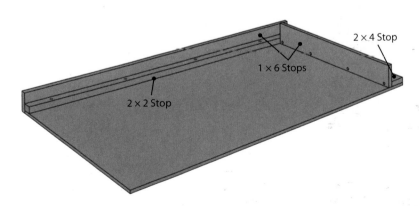

5. ADDING SIDING TO BASIC PANELS.

Set the siding jig on the floor and place the panel on it so the top plate rests flush against the 2-by-2 stop and an outer stud sits against the shorter 1-by-6 stop.

Place a sheet of ⅝-inch exterior siding atop the panel so one end and edge are butted against the 1-by-6 inch stops.

With 2½-inch galvanized box nails, fasten the siding to the top and soleplates and studs, leaving ⅛ inch between panels and driving the fasteners at 6-inch intervals around the perimeter and every 12 inches along the studs (above).

If the panel has a window or door opening, turn it over and drill a hole through the sheathing at each corner of the opening. Join the holes with pencil lines and cut the siding along the marks with a saber saw.

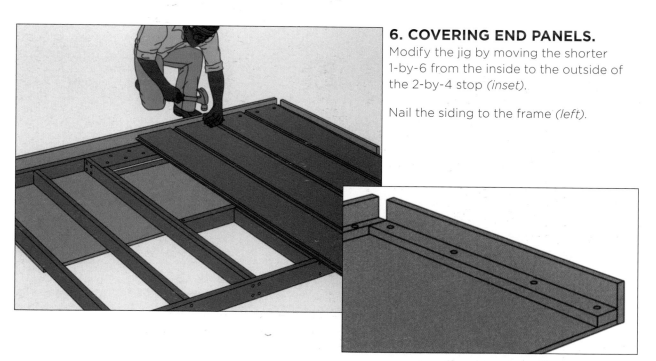

6. COVERING END PANELS.

Modify the jig by moving the shorter 1-by-6 from the inside to the outside of the 2-by-4 stop (inset).

Nail the siding to the frame (left).

7. FLASHING AN OPENING.

With tin snips, cut a piece of 6-inch aluminum flashing to the width of the rough opening.

Bend the aluminum over a 2-by-4 to a 90-degree angle, forming two flanges.

Loosen the siding around the header with a cold chisel or pry bar.

Slip one flange of the flashing between the header and the paneling *(left)*, then nail the flashing and siding to the header.

ERECTING THE PANELS

Nailer Stud

Brace

1. BRACING THE FIRST PANEL.

Have two helpers hold a modified basic panel plumb at one end of the foundation, positioning the nailer stud at the corner.

With 3½-inch common nails, attach a 2-by-4 brace to the second stud, fasten a short board to the bottom of the brace, and nail the board to the subfloor *(above)*.

Fasten a brace at the other end of the panel to hold it plumb.

Anchor the panel to the foundation by nailing its soleplate to the subfloor, driving a nail through the plate between each pair of studs.

EXTENDING THE WALL.

Position the second panel against the first. With a helper holding the panel upright, use a 4-pound maul to align it with the first *(above)*.

Plumb and brace the second panel, then nail the abutting joists of the two panels together.

Repeat the process to raise three of the four walls, working from left to right (when viewed from outside the building) so each corner has a modified panel and an overlapping corner panel.

Bring the interior walls inside, then raise the fourth wall.

With 2-inch galvanized nails, fasten the sheathing of the corner panels to the nailer studs of the modified panels.

Modified Panel

Overlapping Top Plate

Corner Panel

TYING THE WALLS TOGETHER.

Cut a 2-by-4 top plate 4 feet long and, with 3½-inch nails, fasten it atop the top plate of a corner panel so it overlaps the top plate of a modified panel *(left)*.

Continue in this fashion around the perimeter of the wall, nailing on 8-foot-long plates that overlap the seams between adjacent panels. Cut the last 2-by-4 of each wall to fit against the adjoining wall.

Working outside, cover the exposed edges of the siding with 1-by-3s and 1-by-4s fastened with 2¼-inch galvanized finishing nails. Nail on the 1-by-4 first so it overlaps the corner by ¾ inch, then attach the 1-by-3 flush against the 1-by-4.

RAISING PARTITIONS

LOCATING THE WALL.

With a helper at each side wall, snap a chalk line across the subfloor at one side of the proposed wall. To locate a wall directly above the girder, measure the distance between one foundation wall and the girder from below the floor, then transfer the measurement to the floor.

Snap a parallel line 3½ inches from the first *(left)*.

ERECTING THE WALL.

Cut six 2-by-4 blocks to fit between the studs on each side of the chalk lines on the subfloor.

With 3½-inch common nails, fasten three pieces of blocking to each wall, one near the bottom, one at the middle, and one near the top *(right)*.

Raise the interior wall as you did the exterior ones.

Fasten the outer studs of the first and last interior-wall panels to the blocking.

Nail together the end studs of the wall panels, then tie the panels together.

2 × 4 Blocking

INSTALLING A WINDOW

Although it is possible to replace damaged sashes in a window with a sound frame, in some cases you will need to install a new window. Factory-made windows are generally prehung-they include both the sashes that hold the panes of glass and the jambs that make up the window frame.

Choosing a Window: Prehung windows are available in a variety of styles. The most common is the traditional double-hung window in which two sashes slide up and down within the jambs (below). When buying a window, consider its insulating properties, which can be affected by the jamb material and kind of glass in the unit.

Purchase a window that is about ½ inch smaller on all sides than its rough opening to allow for shims to level the unit and for insulation. (If you are framing a new rough opening, choose the window first, then size the opening to accommodate the window.)

Installing the Unit: To install a wood-frame window, nail the jambs to the rough framing through wood shims (opposite); aluminum-and vinyl-frame windows are generally fastened to the outside of the house through a nailing flange around the perimeter of the window. Once the unit is secured in place, insulate the spaces around the jambs with fiberglass or, preferably, a low-expanding foam.

TOOLS
- Hammer
- Carpenter's level
- Spring clamps
- Utility knife
- Nail set
- Putty knife

MATERIALS
- Drip cap
- Finishing nails (3½")
- Galvanized finishing nails (3¼")
- Shims
- Wood putty or spackling compound
- Expanding-foam insulation

FITTING A DOUBLE-HUNG UNIT

1. POSITIONING THE WINDOW.

For a new opening in a wall with wood or vinyl siding, buy a prefabricated drip cap and slip it into place between the siding and the building paper (inset).

Have a helper outside the house set the window in place so it is centered in the opening and the top brickmold fits up under the drip cap (right).

While you hold the window steady from inside, have the helper tack one corner of the top brickmold to the rough-opening header with a 3¼-inch galvanized finishing nail.

Drip Cap

Brickmold

Distance Equal to Thickness of Brickmold

Drip Cap

Building Paper

Rough-Opening Header

Head Jam

Shim

Stud

Horn

Rough Sill

2. LEVELING AND CENTERING THE WINDOW.

Inside, clamp a carpenter's level to the under-side of the head jamb.

While the helper steadies the window from outside, insert shims between the side jambs and studs at the top of the rough opening.

Holding up one corner of the window, slip a shim between the window horn and the rough sill (left). Add a shim under the other horn. Insert additional shims under the horns, as needed, to level the window.

Have your helper nail the other top corner of the brickmold to the header.

Insert shims between the side jambs and the studs at the middle and bottom of the window, being careful not to bow the jambs.

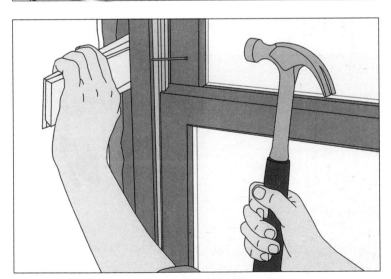

3. NAILING THE WINDOW IN PLACE.

Drive a 3½-inch finishing nail through the side jamb and shims into the stud at each shim location (above). Score the shims along the window jambs with a utility knife, then break them off flush with the jambs. Outside, nail the brick mold to the rough frame every 12 inches with 3¼-inch galvanized finishing nails. Pull the drip cap down tightly against the edge of the head brickmold. With a nail set, sink all the nails.

4. INSULATING WITH FOAM.

Fill the space between the window jambs and the framing with expanding-foam insulation, working from bottom to top when filling the gaps around the sides of the window (above). Use the product sparingly—too much of it can cause the jambs to bow inward when the foam expands.

INSTALLING JAMBS FOR DOORS

Doors are held in their rough openings by a frame called a jamb. If you plan to install a ready-made door, choose a prehung unit, which is supplied with a factory-built jamb. When you build a door to fit an odd-size opening, you will have to make the jamb yourself.

Materials: For interior doors, purchase ¾-inch jamb stock; use 1-or 1½-inch wood for exterior doors. In both cases, the stock should be as wide as the thickness of the wall. Special stock with grooves along the back face will prevent the wood from warping badly with humidity changes.

For the stops *(pages 134-135)* , choose flat stock since you can simply miter it to fit at the corners.

Installing the Jambs: A complete jamb assembly consists of a top and two side pieces joined with special joints called dadoes *(right)*. Here, grooves are cut into the side pieces to accommodate the top piece. You can make these grooves with a router whose bit matches the width of the stock, or you can use a table saw fitted with a dado head. Plan the interior dimensions of the jamb 1 inch wider and higher than the door itself.

For the door to hang properly, the jamb must be perfectly square and plumb- this is achieved by wedging shims between the jamb and the rough opening and making adjustments to them as necessary. If the finish floor is not yet in place, you will also need spacers under the side jambs to hold them until the unit is nailed in place.

TOOLS
- Circular saw
- Router
- Electric drill
- Screwdriver
- Hammer
- Carpenter's level
- Plumb bob
- Utility knife
- Nail set
- Combination square
- Power or manual miter saw

MATERIALS
- Jamb stock
- 1 x 4
- Door stop
- Shims
- Straight board
- Wood screws (1½" No. 8)
- Finishing nails (1½", 3½")
- Wood glue
- Spackling compound or wood putty

MAKING AND FASTENING THE FRAME

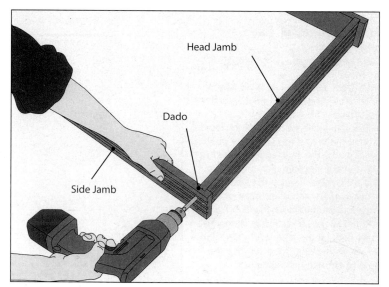

Head Jamb

Dado

Side Jamb

1. ASSEMBLING THE PIECES.
Cut the side jambs slightly shorter than the distance between the finish floor and the top of the rough opening. Make the head jamb ½ inch longer than the desired inside width of the jambs.

Measure along one side jamb a distance equal to the desired height of the jamb opening and make a mark. With a router or table saw, cut a dado ¾ inch wide and ¼ inch deep across the inside face of the jamb at and above this point. Mark and cut a dado on the other side jamb in the same way.

Fit the head jamb into the dado in one of the side jambs and drill pilot holes for two 1½-inch No.8 wood screws. Fasten the jambs together with wood glue and screws. Fasten the head jamb to the other side jamb in the same way *(above)*.

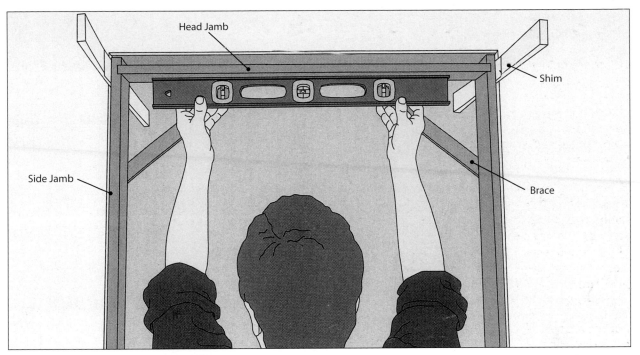

2. POSITIONING THE JAMB.

Tack a brace to the wall diagonally across each top corner of the door opening.

Position the jamb in the opening, propping it against the braces. Cut a 1-by-4 spreader to fit between the side jambs and place it on the floor between the jambs to keep them apart.

Insert pairs of shims on both sides of the door between the side jambs and the rough framing at both ends of the head jamb, adjusting them to center the jamb assembly in the opening.

With a carpenter's level, check the head jamb for level (*above*); if necessary, shift the assembly slightly and adjust the shims.

At the top of each side jamb, drive a 3½-inch finishing nail through the jambs and shims into the rough framing.

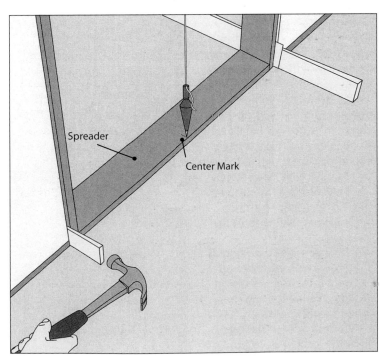

3. CHECKING FOR PLUMB.

Tap pairs of shims between the side jambs and the wall at both ends of the spreader.

Mark the center of the head jamb on its edge and the center of the spreader on its face.

Tack a nail into the edge of the head jamb at the center mark. Hang a plumb bob from the nail so the point of the bob is just above the spreader.

Tap the shims flanking the spreader in or out to align the center mark on the spreader directly under the bob (*left*).

At the bottom of each side jamb, drive a nail through the jamb and shims into the rough framing, then remove the plumb bob, nail, and spreader.

4. SQUARING THE SIDE JAMBS.

Drive additional pairs of shims at the hinge side of the jamb, locating one pair at each planned hinge location (*page 137, Step 1*).

Drive two pairs of shims on the lockset side, locating them just above and below the latch location.

To ensure that the side jambs are straight, press a straight board or a long carpenter's level against one jamb to flatten it and nail through the jamb and shims into the rough framing (*right*). Secure the opposite side jamb in the same way.

Cut off the shims one at a time by holding the end of the shim and slicing across it repeatedly with a utility knife (*inset*) until you can break off the waste piece easily.

With a nail set, sink all the nails; at each hinge location, bury the nails deeper than the thickness of the hinge leaves. If you will be painting the jambs, fill the holes with spackling compound; otherwise, apply wood putty.

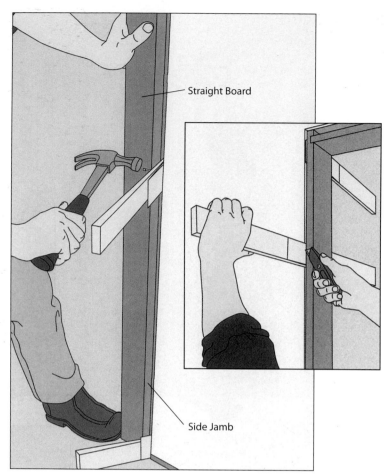

Straight Board

Side Jamb

ADDING STOP MOLDING

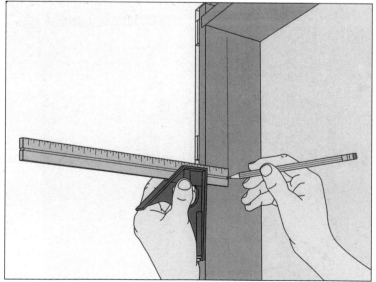

1. LAYING OUT THE DOOR STOPS.

Adjust a combination square to the thickness of the door.

On the side of the jamb that the door will sit flush with when closed, place the handle of the square against the edge of the lockset-side jamb. Set the tip of a pencil against the end of the ruler and run the square down the length of the jamb to mark a guideline for the door stop (*left*).

Mark a guideline on the hinge-side jamb in the same way, but add 1/16 inch to the measurement to prevent the door from binding when it is closed.

2. INSTALLING THE HEAD-JAMB DOOR STOP.

Cut a length of door stop to fit along the head jamb, mitering both ends at 45 degrees with a power or manual miter saw.

Position the stop on the head jamb, aligning the front edge with the guidelines on the side jambs. Tack the stop to the head jamb with 1½-inch finishing nails spaced every 10 to 12 inches and driven only partway in *(right)*.

3. FITTING IN THE SIDE-JAMB STOPS.

Cut two lengths of door stop to fit along the side jambs, mitering the top ends.

Align one stop with the guideline on the lockset-side jamb, holding the end tightly against the head stop. Tack it in place as you did the head-jamb stop *(left)*. Do not drive the nails home or install the hinge-side stop until you have hung the door.

HANGING THE DOOR

Once the jambs are in place, you can install the door. The process involves fitting it to the opening and attaching the hinges.

Fitting the Door: If a ready-made door is too large, you can plane it to fit. A solid door can be trimmed by any amount, but do not remove more than 1 inch from the bottom or sides of a hollow-core type. If you are hanging a shop-made door, you will need to cut a bevel along the lock-set edge *(page 139)*.

Hinges: A solid-core door, or any type taller than 80 inches, requires three hinges. Hollow-core doors or solid ones shorter than the standard can be hung with only two. The size of the hinges depends on the width and thickness of the door *(chart, right)*.

To attach the hinges, you first need to cut shallow insets called mortises in the door and jamb. The best tool for making them is a router *(page 137, Step 1)*. On both the jamb and door, cut the mortises as long as the hinges and ¼ inch narrower than the width of the hinge leaves. When installed, the leaves will extend past the contacting edges of the door and jamb by ¼ inch, preventing the hinges from binding. If you choose hinges with square rather than rounded corners, you will need to chisel out the corners to fit the hinges.

TOOLS

- Saber saw
- Electric drill
- Countersink bit
- Screwdriver
- C-clamps
- Router
- Template guide
- Wood chisel
- Utility knife
- Awl
- Jack plane
- Nail set
- Hammer
- Block plane

MATERIALS

- 1 x 2s
- 2 x 6 scraps
- Plywood (¾")
- Wood blocks
- Wood screws (2" No. 6)
- Common nails (2½")
- Hinges
- Spackling compound or wood putty

CHOOSING HINGES.

Determine the required height of the door hinges according to the width and thickness of the door, as specified in the chart below. The width of the hinges varies with the door's thickness; for a door up to 1⅜ inches thick, you need hinges 3 inches wide; for a 1¾-inch-thick door, 3½-inch-wide hinges are required.

Door Thickness	Door Width	Hinge Height
1⅜"	Up to 32"	3½"-4"
	More than 32"	4"-4½"
1¾"	32"-36"	5"
	36"-48"	5" (heavy-duty type)
	More than 48"	6"

ATTACHING HINGES

1. ROUTING THE JAMB MORTISES.

Purchase a hinge-mortising jig *(right)*, or make a template to guide the router: With a saber saw, cut a piece of ¾-inch plywood about 6 by 12 inches. Make a cutout centered along one edge, cutting it as long as a hinge leaf; for its width, make it as wide as the planned mortise, adding the diameter of the router bit's template guide and ¾ inch for the thickness of the fence. Cut a 2-inch-wide fence the same length as the template and fasten it to the template with four countersunk 2-inch No. 6 wood screws.

Mark the top of the upper hinge on the side jamb by measuring down 7 inches from the head jamb. Mark the bottom of the lowest hinge 11 inches above the bottom of the jamb. If you are adding a third hinge, locate it halfway between the other two.

Clamp the template to the jamb so the fence is against the edge of the jamb on the side where the door will open, and the top of the cutout is aligned with the upper-hinge mark.

Fit the router with a straight bit and template guide, then adjust the depth of cut to the combined thickness of the template and the hinge leaf. With the router flat on the template, move it in small clockwise circles within the template cutout *(right, top)* until the bottom of the mortise is flat.

Reposition the template and rout the middle and bottom mortises.

For rectangular hinges, square the corners of the mortises with a wood chisel.

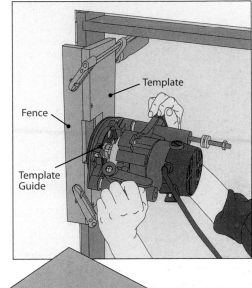

Template
Fence
Template Guide

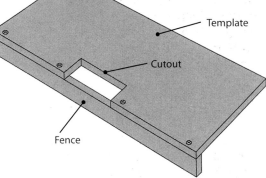

Template
Cutout
Fence

Hinge-Side Jamb
Temporary Shim
Lockset-Side Jamb

2. TRANSFERRING THE HINGE LOCATIONS.

Working with a helper, prop the door in its frame.

With your helper holding 2½-inch nails as spacers between the top of the door and the head jamb, drive wood blocks under the door to wedge it tight against the nails.

Drive a shim between the door and the lockset-side jamb about 3 feet from the floor to push the door against the hinge-side jamb.

With a utility knife, nick the edge of the door at the top and bottom of each hinge mortise in the jamb *(left)*.

Rout the hinge mortises on the door.

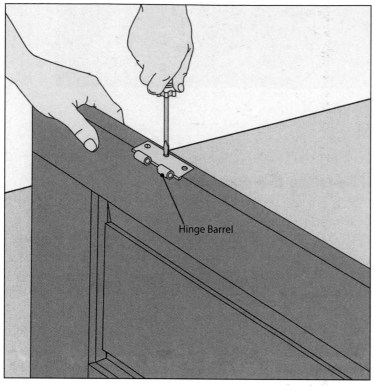

3. ATTACHING THE HINGES.

Separate the two leaves of a hinge by pulling out the pin. Set the leaf with two barrels in a mortise on the door and mark the screw holes with an awl.

Remove the hinge leaf, drill pilot holes for the screws provided, and fasten the leaf to the door *(left)*.

Install the other hinges on the door in the same way, then attach the matching leaves to the jamb.

Hinge Barrel

A HINGE-MORTISING JIG

A commercial hinge-mortising jig has templates to fit three different hinge sizes and spacings. Adaptable to doors either 1⅜ or 1¾ inches thick, the jig can be used for mortises on both the jamb and the door. In the model shown here, plastic spacers are inserted in the jig to change the size of the hinge cavity.

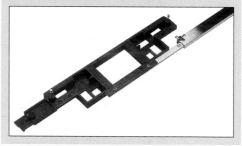

4. HANGING THE DOOR TEMPORARILY.

Lift the door into position and slip some wood blocks under it. Shift the door to engage the barrels of the top hinge, then slide the hinge pin in partway *(left)*.

Pivot the door to join the bottom hinge leaves and slip the hinge pin in partway, then fit the pin in the middle hinge.

5. MARKING THE BEVEL.

Standing on the door-stop side, close the door—its front edge will hit the edge of the jamb, preventing it from closing fully.

Holding the door against the jamb, scribe a pencil line down the face of the door where it meets the jamb *(right)*.

Jamb

6. BEVELING THE DOOR EDGE.

With a ruler, extend the pencil line across the ends of the door, marking the angle of the bevel.

Holding a jack plane at the same angle, guide it along the door edge *(left)*. A portable power planer that can be set to the desired bevel angle—3 to 5 degrees—is also handy for this job.

Continue planing until you reach the pencil line.

Rehang the door as in Step 4, inserting the hinge pins all the way this time. Install the hinge-side door stop, butting it against the head-jamb stop *(page 135, Step 3)*.

Pass a dime along the hinge jamb to check for the correct clearance between it and the door; use a nickel to check the clearance at the top and other side of the door. If necessary, take the door down again and plane any high spots. Use a block plane for the top or bottom of the door, working from the edges toward the center to avoid splintering the end grain.

When the door fits properly, drive all the nails home and sink them with a nail set, then fill the holes.

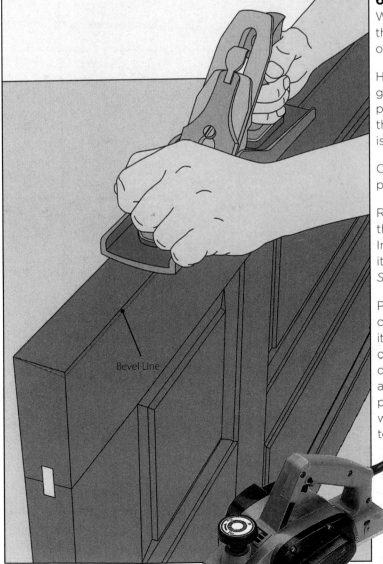

Bevel Line

FINISHING UP WITH TRIM

The final step in installing the door is to add casing. This molding hides the gap between the jamb and the wallboard, and gives the door a finished look.

Casing Styles: It's best to use the same style of molding for the door as for the windows in the room. If stool-and-apron trim was applied around the windows, make butt joints in the door casing *(below)*. For a room with windows trimmed in picture-frame style, miter the corners of the door molding following the same technique.

Preparing the Jamb: Since the casing links the jamb and the wall, these two surfaces must be flush. If the jamb is slightly proud of the wall, plane it down. Where it is slightly shy of the wall, shave down the wallboard with a rasp; but if the jamb is set back more than 1 inch from the wall, make and install a jamb extension of the same type used for a stool-and-apron window.

ATTACHING THE CASING

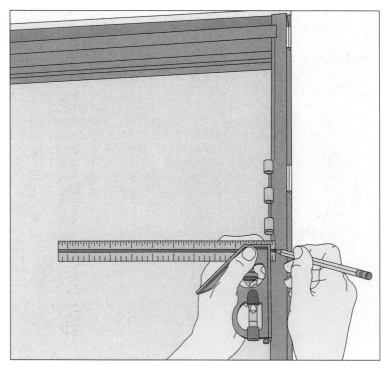

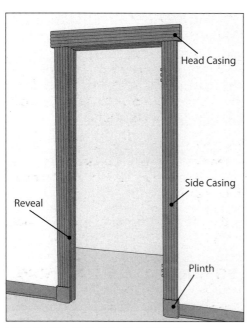

BUTTED DOOR CASING

In this classic casing style, side and head casing meet with a simple butt joint, and the head casing overhangs the side casing by about 1 inch at each end. The inside edges of the casing are off-set from those of the jambs, leaving a 1-inch reveal. Decorative rosettes can be added at the top corners if desired.

Rather than resting on the floor, the side casing usually rests on a pair of plinth blocks slightly thicker and wider than the casing and 1 inch taller than the baseboard.

1. MARKING THE REVEAL.

Remove the door.

Set a combination square to ¼ inch, checking that this is wide enough to clear the hinges. Butting the handle of the square against the face of a side jamb and resting a pencil against the end of the ruler, mark a reveal line the length of the jamb edge *(above)*.

Mark the same reveal on the other side jamb as well as on the head jamb.

2. FASTENING THE PLINTHS.

Cut two plinth blocks to the desired height and width. If desired, bevel one edge of the blocks with a power or manual miter saw; to cut larger stock with a power saw, you may need a compound miter saw.

Align the edge of a block with the reveal line—if the finish flooring is not yet in place, set a scrap of wood the thickness of the flooring under the plinth block.

Nail the plinth block to the jamb and to the rough framing.

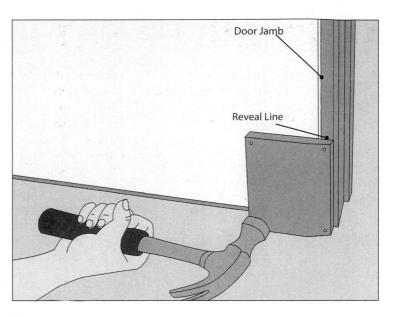

3. ATTACHING THE HEAD CASING.

Measure the distance between the reveal lines on the two side jambs. Add to this figure the width of both of the side casings to be used plus 1½ inches and cut the head casing to this length.

Mark the center of the head jamb and the head casing. Align the head casing with the reveal mark and line up the two center marks.

Nail the casing to the jamb and the rough framing.

4. FITTING IN THE SIDE CASING.

Cut the side casings to fit snugly between the plinths and head casing.

Fit one piece into position, aligning it with the reveal line *(left)*. Fasten it in the same way as the head casing, then put up the other side piece.

With a nail set, sink all the nails. If you plan to paint the casing, fill the holes with spackling compound; otherwise use wood putty.

FOUR LIGHTS TINY HOUSE COMPANY

LICENSE AGREEMENT

The term "Licensed Product" is herein defined as a set of plans purchased from Four Lights Tiny House Co. "Licensed Product" does NOT refer to this book. Purchase of the book does NOT include a license to build any of the designs shown in the book.

IMPORTANT READ CAREFULLY: This License Agreement (the "Agreement") is a legal agreement between you and Four Lights Tiny House Company, a California company with a principal business address of PO Box 239, Cotati, CA 94931 (hereinafter "Licensor," "we," or "us"). By using the Licensed Product, you agree to be bound by the terms of this Agreement. If you do not agree to the terms of this Agreement, then you should not use the Licensed Product. You should also read the full text describing the risks below and accept and acknowledge the risks before you use the Licensed Product in accordance with this Agreement. Either of us may be referred to individually as a "Party" or collectively as the "Parties."

Please be advised: this license is intended for the construction of a structure for personal use or for internal use by a single business. This license expressly prohibits construction for commercial resale.

1. OUR PLANS

We recommend consulting with a licensed contractor prior to attempting to build the Licensed Product. Our plans have not been checked for compliance with the particular codes or conditions in your area. We recommend that you consult with your local building officials before installing any new structure, in order to ensure that your house will comply with local building codes.

2. INTELLECTUAL PROPERTY IN THE PLANS

We shall retain all right, title, and interest to the intellectual property, trade secrets, and know-how in the Licensed Product ("Intellectual Property"). You acknowledge that no title to or rights in the Intellectual Property are transferred to you from us under this Agreement. You agree not to remove any trademark, copyright, or other proprietary notices on or in any portion of the Licensed Product as delivered and to reproduce all such notices on all authorized copies.

3. LICENSE

We grant to you a royalty-free, non-exclusive, nontransferable license solely for your individual use or internal business use (a) to use the Licensed Product; (b) to create up to five (5) hard copies of the Licensed Product for your personal or your internal business use only; (c) to construct a structure based upon the Licensed Product for your personal use or internal business use only; and (d) to customize the Licensed Product for your personal or internal business use only. Your rights in the Licensed Product shall be limited to those expressly granted in this Agreement. Any use which exceeds the scope of this license grant shall be deemed to constitute a material breach of this Agreement, including but not limited to using the Licensed Product for commercial resale purposes.

4. RESTRICTIONS

You shall not distribute, share, rent, resell, lease, sublicense, reproduce, or otherwise disclose or transfer the Licensed Product to any third party. You shall not use the Licensed Product in any other multiple use arrangement, or allow third parties to have access to the Licensed Product. You shall not use the Licensed Product for commercial resale purposes, make more than five (5) hard copies of the Licensed Product, share any copies of the Licensed Product with third parties, or permit the Licensed Product to be used by any third party for commercial resale purposes. You shall not share any customizations you have made to the Licensed Product with any third party or use those customizations for any commercial resale purposes, nor shall you permit any third party to disassemble or reverse engineer your structure after it is constructed. Notwithstanding the foregoing, you are authorized to distribute up to five (5) hard copies to contractors building a structure for your own purposes or for the internal purposes of your business; provided that, however, such contractors may not use the Licensed Product to build any structure other than one that you will use and they must they return or destroy all hard copies upon completion of the work.

Any failure to abide by the restrictions set forth in this Section shall expressly constitute a material breach of this Agreement.

5. TERM; TERMINATION

This Agreement commences as of the date on which you purchase the book in which these plans are published ("Effective Date") and is perpetual. This Agreement will automatically terminate upon notice in the event you materially breach any term or condition of this Agreement. You understand that exceeding the scope of the license shall expressly constitute a material breach of this Agreement. Upon any material breach, your non-exclusive license shall cease and terminate, and you shall have no further right to access use, display, print, reproduce, or make copies of the Licensed Product. The following terms and conditions shall survive any termination: Sections 2,4, 5, and 7-10.

6. DISCLAIMER OF OTHER WARRANTIES

The Licensed Product is provided on an "as is" basis. Use of the Licensed Product is at your own risk. You solely assume any and all risks with respect to the construction of your house based on the Licensed Product. We can make no warranty that the Licensed Product will meet all of your needs or result in a successful or satisfactory outcome for you, nor can we warrant that the Licensed Product will be completely accurate, current, complete, or free from errors and omissions. We can make no warranty that the Licensed Product will comply with the particular codes or conditions in your area, nor can we warrant that your actual costs will not vary from our estimated building costs. TO THE EXTENT PERMITTED BY LAW AND EXCEPT AS EXPRESSLY PROVIDED IN THE LIMITED WARRANTY SET FORTH ABOVE, WE EXPRESSLY DISCLAIM ALL OTHER WARRANTIES, CONDITIONS, RESULTS, GUARANTEES, OR REPRESENTATIONS WITH RESPECT TO THE LICENSED PRODUCT, WHETHER EXPRESS OR IMPLIED, INCLUDING BUT NOT LIMITED TO THE IMPLIED WARRANTIES OF MERCHANTABILITY, MERCHANTABLE OR SATISFACTORY QUALITY, FITNESS FOR A PARTICULAR PURPOSE, NONINFRINGEMENT OF THIRD PARTY RIGHTS, OR ARISING FROM THE COURSE OF PERFORMANCE, COURSE OF DEALING, OR USAGE OF TRADE.

7. REMEDIES

Upon receipt of written notice from you of a physical defect in the delivery of the Licensed Product, our entire liability and your sole and exclusive remedy shall be to receive a replacement delivery of the Licensed Product at no charge.

8. INDEMNIFICATION

You agree to indemnify, defend, and hold harmless us, our officers, directors, employees, independent contractors, representatives, and agents from and against any and all loss, damage liability, and expense (including without limitation reasonable fees for attorneys and experts) arising out of any claim, demand, cause of action, debt or liability, including reasonable attorneys' fees, to the extent that such action is based upon a claim that (a) if true, would constitute a breach of any representations or agreements by you hereunder; (b) arises out of any negligence or willful misconduct by you; (c) you have infringed our intellectual property rights hereunder; or (d) is based on any third party claim that arises out of this Agreement.

9. MISCELLANEOUS

In no event shall we be liable for any incidental, consequential, indirect, special, or punitive damages, or lost profits, arising out of, or related to, this Agreement, even if we have been advised of the possibility thereof, and regardless of whether the claim is based on contract, tort, or another theory or cause of action. If any provision of this Agreement is held unenforceable or in conflict with the law of any jurisdiction, the validity of the remaining provisions shall not be affected. The meaning of that provision will be construed to the extent feasible, to render the provision unenforceable.

10. GOVERNING LAW; DISPUTE RESOLUTION

This Agreement is governed by the laws of the State of California, without regard to conflicts of law principles. All disputes arising under this Agreement shall be submitted to binding arbitration in San Francisco, CA under the Commercial Rules of the American Arbitration Association by one arbitrator mutually agreed upon both you and us in accordance with the aforementioned Rules.

Should you have any questions about this Agreement, of if you desire to contact us for any reason, all communications should be directed to: Four Lights Tiny House Company, PO Box 239, Cotati, CA 94931.

More Great Books from Fox Chapel Publishing

Wood Pallet Projects
ISBN 978-1-56523-544-1 **$19.99**

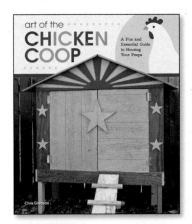

Art of the Chicken Coop
ISBN 978-1-56523-542-7 **$19.95**

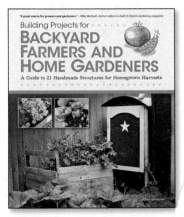

**Building Projects for Backy
Farmers and Home Garder**
ISBN 978-1-56523-543-4 **$19.**

Metal Working
ISBN 978-1-56523-540-3 **$19.95**

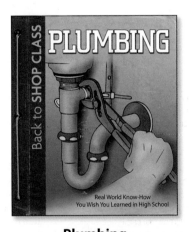

Plumbing
ISBN 978-1-56523-588-5 **$19.95**

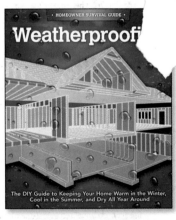

Weatherproofing
ISBN 978-1-56523-591-5 **$19.95**

Masonry
ISBN 978-1-56523-698-1 **$24.95**

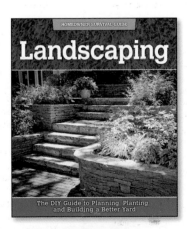

Landscaping
ISBN 978-1-56523-699-8 **$24.95**

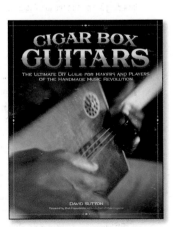

Cigar Box Guitars
ISBN 978-1-56523-547-2 **$29.95**

THE SMALL HOUSE BOOK
JAY SHAFER

Discover 22 brilliant small home plans you can build, created by America's leading designer of the Small House Movement.